The Fullness of the Holy Spirit
In You - For You - With You

Dr. Bob Abramson

The Fullness of the Holy Spirit In You - For You - With You

Published by Alphabet Resources, Inc.
365 Stonehenge Drive
Phillipsburg, NJ 08865
1-561-963-0778
Dr.Bob@mentoringministry.com

Cover design by Ryan Stacey - Visual Lion

13 digit ISBN 978-0-9846580-4-6

Contact Dr. Abramson by visiting
www.mentoringministry.com.

Preface

In this book, I have done my best to provide an accurate representation of many issues concerning the Holy Spirit and His nine spiritual gifts to the church (1 Corinthians, Chapters 12 and 14.) I am pleased to begin with the following thoughts on what it means to be filled with the Holy Spirit. They are from a sermon by Reverend Phillip Bedwell.[1] He has graciously given his permission to quote from it.

> "To be filled with the Spirit means to exclude sin and then to include the power and presence of the Holy Spirit. It means the infusion of the presence of the Spirit. It has been said by one Bible scholar that the word filled in the original language of the Scripture is used in three ways. We have already said that it meant more than the filling up of a container. The Holy Spirit is not to be thought of as a Divine fluid with which our hearts may be filled. The word filled was often used of the wind filling the sail and thereby carrying the ship along. To be filled with the Holy Spirit is to be moved along by the power and inspiration of the Holy Spirit just as the writers of the scriptures were moved by the Holy Spirit. The [term] filled was also used of salt which permeated the meat in order that it might keep its flavor

---

[1] With permission, of Rev. Phillip Bedwell, Bedwell Global Ministries, www.Innercourt.co.za/main/page.

i

as well [as] preserve it. To be filled with the Spirit of God is to have His glorious presence saturate, penetrate and pervade our lives so that they reflect the beauty of a Christlike character. But thirdly the word filled also has the connotation of total control or complete authority."

Reverend Bedwell concludes with the following:

"The teaching of the New Testament assumes being filled with the Spirit is imperative. It leaves no room for an option. Indeed the Christian life cannot be lived victoriously and in true holiness without the fullness of the Spirit. Each child of God needs the presence of the Holy Spirit in this way. Jesus said "without me you can nothing." There are so many who are living between Easter and Pentecost. They have received the living Christ into their lives, but have yet to surrender to the Baptism of the Holy Spirit. The fullness which the Baptism of the Spirit brings to the soul is being ignored by many and the result is ineffective witnesses and defeated living and a powerless church. For the shooting of the film Ben Hur, Charlton Heston was training to drive a chariot. Charlton was having trouble with his equipment and so he confided in his director, William Wyler. He said "I can barely stay on this thing. I can't win the race." Wyler told Heston, "Your job is stay on it. It is my job to make sure you win." That is the function of the Holy Spirit in your life and mine. The power of His presence ensures that we will win."

Table of Contents

Part One: The Fullness of the Holy Spirit... In You

INTRODUCTION   3

ONE   The Beginning of Constant Access   9

TWO   The Demonstration of Constant Access   17

THREE   The Power of Constant Access   27

FOUR   Fire from Heaven   37

FIVE   Wisdom from God   49

SIX   Guarding Your Access to God's Wisdom   57

SEVEN   Uncommon Sense   71

EIGHT   Uncommon Love   77

NINE   Uncommon Commitment   89

TWENTY-SIX THOUGHTS ON THE HOLY SPIRIT... IN YOU   95

Part Two: The Nine Gifts of the Holy Spirit... For You

TEN   An Introduction to the Nine Gifts... For You   101

ELEVEN   The Three Revelation Gifts... For You   115

TWELVE   The Three Power Gifts... For You   125

THIRTEEN   The Three Vocal/Utterance Gifts... For You   137
             The First Gift: PROPHECY

FOURTEEN   The Three Vocal/Utterance Gifts... For You   151
             The Second and Third Gifts: DIFFERENT KINDS
             OF TONGUES and INTERPRETATION OF TONGUES

Part Three: The Holy Spirit... With You

FIFTEEN   Comforter, Helper, Counselor   167

SIXTEEN   A Journey of Your Choosing   175

SEVENTEEN   A Demonstration of the Spirit and Power   185

EIGHTEEN   Revealed Through His Spirit   193

NINETEEN   Comparing Spiritual Things with Spiritual   201

TWENTY   Blessed with the Spirit... For a Purpose   209

About Dr. Abramson   217

Part One

The Fullness of the Holy Spirit... In You

INTRODUCTION

Galatians 5:16-18 (NKJV)

"I say then: Walk in the Spirit, and you shall not fulfill the lust of the flesh. {17} For the flesh lusts against the Spirit, and the Spirit against the flesh; and these are contrary to one another, so that you do not do the things that you wish. {18} But if you are led by the Spirit, you are not under the law."

In Chapter 5 of his Epistle to the Galatians, the Apostle Paul gave us contrasting images of the two ways in which we can go through our daily lives - in the *"Spirit"* or in the *"flesh."* A simple way to understand this is to look at the biblically-based difference between *"walking in the Spirit"* and walking in the *"lust of the flesh."* These terms are absolutely contrary to one another. On the following page, I have illustrated the difference between these two ways of living by posing the question, "Are You Walking in the Flesh or the Spirit?" As you read this, notice the stark scriptural contrast between the two ways of living.

Are You Walking in the Flesh or the Spirit?

Galatians 5:19-25 (NKJV)

Walking in the Flesh (Living in ways that *"fulfill the lust of the flesh"*)		Walking in the Spirit (Living in ways that result in fruitfulness in God's kingdom)
{19}	*"Now the works of the flesh are evident, which are: adultery, fornication, uncleanness, lewdness,*	
{20}	*idolatry, sorcery, hatred, contentions, jealousies, outbursts of wrath, selfish ambitions, dissensions, heresies,*	
{21}	*envy, murders, drunkenness, revelries, and the like; of which I tell you beforehand, just as I also told you in time past, that <u>those who practice such things will not inherit the kingdom of God</u>.*	
{22}		*But the fruit of the Spirit is love, joy, peace, longsuffering, kindness, goodness, faithfulness,*
{23}		*gentleness, self-control. Against such there is no law.*
{24-25}	*And those who are Christ's have crucified the flesh with its passions and desires. {25} If we live in the Spirit, let us also walk in the Spirit."*	

Walking Worthy of the Lord

As you have seen from the Scriptures, when we walk in the Spirit, our lives bear fruit that is *"fully pleasing"* to the Lord. This fruitfulness is reflected in who we are and in all that we do for God. Paul reinforced this in his Epistle to the Colossians.

Colossians 1:10 (NKJV)

"...that you may walk worthy of the Lord, fully pleasing Him, being fruitful in every good work and increasing in the knowledge of God,"

Paul used the expression, *"that you may walk worthy of the Lord..."* We will discuss this in detail in another chapter, but what Paul described was a liberating walk filled with potential. The word *"worthy"* describes something that is commendable and even precious in the sight of someone watching.

Walking in the Spirit is Vital to Every Christian.

God gives every Christian the right and the opportunity to walk *"according to the Spirit."*

Romans 8:1-5 (NKJV)

"There is therefore now no condemnation to those who are in Christ Jesus, who do not walk according to the flesh, but according to the Spirit. {2} For the law of the Spirit of life in Christ Jesus has made me free from the law of sin and death.

5

{3} For what the law could not do in that it was weak through the flesh, God did by sending His own Son in the likeness of sinful flesh, on account of sin: He condemned sin in the flesh, {4} that the righteous requirement of the law might be fulfilled in us who do not walk according to the flesh but according to the Spirit. {5} For those who live according to the flesh set their minds on the things of the flesh, but those who live according to the Spirit, the things of the Spirit."

Paul encouraged the people of the church at Rome to recognize the value of the position they enjoyed in Christ. No longer were they condemned by their sins. Now, because Christ was their Lord and Savior, they could walk in an attitude of liberty. They were free of condemnation and the power of sin. They were free of eternal death. Now (as Paul wrote in Romans 8:5), they could have attitudes based on the things that the Holy Spirit brought to their minds. Their actions could reflect these attitudes. They could think as free people. They could experience life, acting in ways that were worthy of the Lord. These truths are valid for today. Walking worthy of the Lord is our great opportunity. It is God's goal for each of us. As we do, we fulfill His purposes.

Paul's Clear Warning

Ephesians 4:17-21 (NKJV)

"This I say, therefore, and testify in the Lord, that you should no longer walk as the rest of the Gentiles walk, in the futility of their mind, {18}

having their understanding darkened, being alienated from the life of God, because of the ignorance that is in them, because of the blindness of their heart; {19} who, being past feeling, have given themselves over to lewdness, to work all uncleanness with greediness. {20} But you have not so learned Christ, {21} if indeed you have heard Him and have been taught by Him, as the truth is in Jesus:"

In Ephesians 4:17-21, Paul reminded his readers that they were no longer to be living a carnal life. They were now to be living spiritual lives. Their minds should not be filled with carnal thinking. Paul's words teach us that, as God's people, our lives should no longer be darkened by ignorance and sin. We have been taught the truth about Jesus. Because of this, it is our responsibility to be living demonstrations of maturity and grace. We are to be worthy (and walk worthy) of the Lord who saved us. His Holy Spirit will accompany us, every step of the way.

A Great Step Forward

Now that we have established what it means to be walking in the Spirit, we can move forward to learn the significance of living in *"the fullness"* of the Holy Spirit. This term, *"fullness"* means realizing the potential of the vast capabilities that the Holy Spirit can provide to us. Living this way is a great step forward beyond where most of us normally live. Though living in the fullness of the Holy

Spirit is available to all of God's people, it is a choice we each must make in order to enjoy this level of spiritual life.

In the following chapters, we will explore the value in taking ourselves to new levels of the Spirit-led experience. We will discover the unlimited boundaries of liberty that a full life in the Holy Spirit brings. We will look at the blessings available as we make this journey in Christ. We will see the opportunity to fulfill our destinies, going from *"glory to glory."*

2 Corinthians 3:17-18 (NKJV)

"Now the Lord is the Spirit; and where the Spirit of the Lord is, there is liberty. {18} But we all, with unveiled face, beholding as in a mirror the glory of the Lord, are being transformed into the same image from glory to glory, just as by the Spirit of the Lord."

Questions for Discussion

1. Why do so many people fail to overcome certain lusts of the flesh?

2. Define *"walking worthy of the Lord"* in your own words.

3. What are some personal goals you can set for stepping beyond where you are now, spiritually?

ONE

The Beginning of Constant Access

Walking in the Spirit ought to be a vital part of every Christian's lifestyle. It causes God-pleasing actions, which lead us to personal growth. Personal growth invites personal fruitfulness. This chapter will challenge you with these questions: Is there something more? Can we find a level of walking in the Holy Spirit that takes us beyond where we are today? Can we find a fullness in this experience that provides us with additional, measurable benefits and blessings? If so, how can we get to this level? Below, is a list of four attributes that help define "walking in the fullness of the Holy Spirit." As Christians, these attributes can be goals, embraced by all who desire to walk more fully in God's Spirit. They will be covered in Chapters 1-9. They can be divided into four categories:

1. Constant Access to the Holy Spirit

2. Constant Access to Extreme God-sourced Power

3. Constant Access to Spiritual Wisdom and Understanding

4. Constant Access to the "Uncommon."

Each of these four attributes holds the potential to be unrestrained and without limits within us. Each can touch and affect the eternities of those we encounter in life.

The Prayer of Potential

In his First Epistle to the Corinthians, Paul wrote that they were to imitate him in the same ways he imitated Christ (1 Corinthians 11:1). God has placed within us the same potential to imitate Christ without measure or limit. Paul may have had this limitless potential in mind when he wrote this prayer to the Colossians.

Colossians 1:9-11 (NKJV)

"For this reason we also, since the day we heard it, do not cease to pray for you, and to ask that you may be filled with the knowledge of His will in all wisdom and spiritual understanding; {10} that you may walk worthy of the Lord, fully pleasing Him, being fruitful in every good work and increasing in the knowledge of God; {11} strengthened with all might, according to His glorious power, for all patience and longsuffering with joy;"

Colossians 1:9-11 is a prayer of potential. What does it teach, regarding the principle of unlimited potential for "walking in the fullness of the Holy Spirit?" Does this prayer help us answer what this level of *"fullness"* means? Consider these words, below, that are taken from Paul's prayer to the Colossians:

Verse 9: *"filled"*
Verse 9: *"all"* (again in Verse 11)
Verse 10: *"fully"*

Paul saw the potential in God's people for more than the normal Christian experience. He saw the opportunity for us to live a complete spiritual life by accessing the *"fullness"* of the experience. He saw it as an abundant life without measure.

- It contains *"all"* God has to offer.
- It carries the potential to be a life *"filled"* with God.
- It is a walk in the Holy Spirit that will be *"fully pleasing Him."*

Now, as we build a picture of what a *"fully pleasing"* life in God looks like, let's begin with the first attribute of walking in the fullness of the Holy Spirit. Let's look at constant access to Him.

Constant Access Defined

Access may be defined as follows:
- The ability or right to enter (a place) or use (something)
- The right or opportunity to approach or speak with[2]
- Access may also describe an unencumbered, open path.

As Christians, we have the born-again birthright and opportunity to have constant access to the Holy Spirit, throughout each moment of our daily lives. This right is available to all of us, and happens when we do the following:

1. We stay persistently close to the Holy Spirit throughout the day.

---

[2] Webster's College Dictionary - Word Genius.

11

2. We deliberately include Him and defer to His voice in everything possible.

3. We imitate others who imitate Christ. Make it part of the patterns of your life to imitate those who access God's Spirit in a constant, extraordinary way, without limitations or measure.

> A great example of a man who has an extraordinary measure of access to God's Spirit is Pastor Suli Kurulo, the President of the Christian Mission Fellowship in Fiji. He began his ministry many years ago and found himself walking in this extraordinary measure of the fullness of the Holy Spirit, throughout the islands of Fiji. He preached the Gospel in every village, town and city. He and his disciples reached every home in the nation. In doing this, they suffered great persecution. Through it all, Pastor Suli hungered for and maintained constant access to the Holy Spirit. As a result, people began to come to Christ.
>
> Pastor Suli's determined desire for access brought him to places in ministry far beyond what he expected in the beginning. It also brought him greater vision for what was in God's heart for the world. He has been a world-changer and one of the devil's worst nightmares. There are thousands of South Pacific missionaries, now living and working on all the inhabited continents of the world. This happened because Pastor Suli maintained his desire for unrestrained, unlimited, endless access to the

Holy Spirit. He took advantage of his position in Christ and continues to fulfill the will of God for his life.

4. We make the first three reasons consistent, disciplined habits of our daily lives. They form a pattern, a constant way of living.

Hearing the Voice of the Holy Spirit

Constant access to the Holy Spirit has these three advantages. It allows us to hear His voice (1) more easily, (2) more completely and (3) more clearly. This does not happen automatically. It requires effort to gain and maintain it. Let's look at these three advantages.

1. HEARING MORE EASILY

Hearing the Holy Spirit more easily only occurs with determined practice. Through the years, one of the most common questions I have been asked is how to hear the voice of God more easily. Too many Christians struggle with this. The answer is simply to keep listening. We know God speaks to us through His Word, but there are many other ways He speaks to us. You can hear Him in your thoughts. You can hear Him by carefully observing your circumstances. You can hear Him when others speak and He provides a message through their words. On occasion, He might choose to speak audibly and directly to you. His desire is that you hear Him without restraints or limits. He wants to communicate with you even more than you do with Him.

2. HEARING MORE COMPLETELY

The key to hearing more completely is patience. We often hear a part of what He tells us and assume it is the complete message. This is not always true. He may speak to us in a series of messages before we can fully understand what He is saying. The key to hearing more completely is to exercise patience as you listen for what He says. (Remember, His message can come in any combination of the ways you just read, concerning hearing Him more easily.)

3. HEARING MORE CLEARLY

This skill can be learned by focusing on Him, and not becoming distracted. Distraction is the enemy of listening. If you desire to hear the Holy Spirit more clearly, you must have the attitude that what He says is what is most important to you. His words will lead and guide you. They will protect you. They will show you the things you need to know, so you can succeed in what you need to do. Focus on Him and He will focus on you. The Holy Spirit desires that you and He have a focused relationship. I believe this was the reason Pastor Suli became (and continues to be) so effective and influential. He knows the value of having a focused relationship with the Holy Spirit.

At the beginning of this chapter, you were asked to consider these questions: Can we find a level of walking in the Holy Spirit that exceeds the normal Christian life? Can we find a fullness of the experience that provides us with additional, measurable benefits and blessings? If so, how can we get to this level? The answers all begin with access to His Spirit. Access brings us closer to Him and to His will. Look again at Colossians 1:10. Below, I have provided the New Living Translation for you. It gives a descriptive, encouraging picture of the results of access to the Holy Spirit.

Colossians 1:10 (NLT)

"Then the way you live will always honor and please the Lord, and you will continually do good, kind things for others. All the while, you will learn to know God better and better."

The New Living Translation shows us that access results in the following advantages and blessings:

1. You will consistently honor and please God. This will lead you to achieving unrestrained, unlimited and positive outcomes.

2. In the eyes of God, the things that you do will be *"good."* They will bear eternal fruitfulness for God's kingdom. This means your ability to be a positive influence will be enhanced greatly through your access to the Holy Spirit.

3. Your access will be so strong and constant that you will learn to know God more intimately every day.

Living at a normal level is for anyone. God has destined your life to be lived at the highest level.

Questions for Discussion

1. How would you define *"walking in the fullness of the Holy Spirit,"* using your own thoughts and words?

2. What would you say is the most important reason some people have greater, fuller access to the Holy Spirit than others do?

3. What would you say is the most important reason many people struggle with increasing their access to the Holy Spirit?

TWO

The Demonstration of Constant Access

(Unrestrained, Unlimited and Endless)

Let's begin this chapter by reviewing the meanings of "access."
- The ability or right to enter (a place) or use (something)
- The right or opportunity to approach or speak with[3]
- Access may also describe an unencumbered, open path.

As you read in the previous chapter, three advantages of constant access to the Holy Spirit are: (1) We can hear His voice more easily. (2) We can hear His voice more completely. (3) We can hear His voice more clearly. Hearing the voice of the Holy Spirit does not happen automatically. It requires effort to gain and maintain access to what He is saying. We will begin to look at what access to *"walking in the fullness of the Holy Spirit"* means.

The Lord's Example

Luke 4:1-2 (NKJV)

"Then Jesus, being filled with the Holy Spirit, returned from the Jordan and was led by the Spirit

---

[3] Webster's College Dictionary - Word Genius.

into the wilderness, {2} being tempted for forty days by the devil. And in those days He ate nothing, and afterward, when they had ended, He was hungry."

Luke 4:13-15 (NKJV)

"Now when the devil had ended every temptation, he departed from Him until an opportune time. {14} Then Jesus returned in the power of the Spirit to Galilee, and news of Him went out through all the surrounding region. {15} And He taught in their synagogues, being glorified by all."

Jesus walked into and out of the desert in the fullness of His relationship with the Holy Spirit. (This is an excellent model, which we should strive to achieve, especially when temptation tries to capture us.) Following His temptation by the devil in the wilderness, Jesus returned to Galilee. The Bible says He was filled with the Holy Spirit's power. He then went to Nazareth and was in the temple on the Sabbath. In the temple, He was asked to teach. Luke 4:18-19 records that He stood up and quoted from Isaiah 61. He told those present that Isaiah's prophetic words were fulfilled on that very day. Here is what He said:

Luke 4:18-19 (NKJV)

"The Spirit of the LORD is upon Me, Because He has anointed Me To preach the gospel to the poor; He has sent Me to heal the brokenhearted, To proclaim liberty to the captives And recovery of

sight to the blind, To set at liberty those who are oppressed; {19} To proclaim the acceptable year of the LORD."

Jesus' life fully demonstrated what He had proclaimed. Demonstration of God's Word is now our model to follow. We are to give evidence of the quality of our access to the Holy Spirit. We are to give testimony of this access by demonstrating it. Our Spirit-led actions are to be anointed, unrestrained, and without limits, as to what they can accomplish. The results will manifest themselves with eternal value and fruitfulness.

What is your attitude about walking in the fullness of the Holy Spirit? In Romans, Paul asked us to change our attitudes (the ways we think) so our actions will show the world *"the perfect will of God."*

Romans 12:1-2 (NKJV)

"I beseech you therefore, brethren, by the mercies of God, that you present your bodies a living sacrifice, holy, acceptable to God, which is your reasonable service. {2} And do not be conformed to this world, but be transformed by the renewing of your mind, that you may prove what is that good and acceptable and perfect will of God."

Paul understood that we all have the potential to have unrestrained, unlimited, eternal relationships with the Holy Spirit. When this becomes the pattern of our lives, everything else God desires for us will follow. With God,

19

nothing is impossible and everything is possible. Refuse to accept the impossible. The fullness of the Holy Spirit in your life will make all things possible.

There are many biblical examples of people who demonstrated access to the Holy Spirit. The examples occur in both testaments. Here are a few that teach us about the reality of having access to Him.

Samuel's Example

1 Samuel 3:8-10 (NLT)

"So now the LORD called a third time, and once more Samuel jumped up and ran to Eli. "Here I am," he said. "What do you need?" Then Eli realized it was the LORD who was calling the boy. {9} So he said to Samuel, "Go and lie down again, and if someone calls again, say, 'Yes, LORD, your servant is listening.'" So Samuel went back to bed. {10} And the LORD came and called as before, "Samuel! Samuel!" And Samuel replied, "Yes, your servant is listening.""

Samuel's access to the voice of the Holy Spirit began when he was a small child. It lasted throughout his lifetime. He heard the voice of God often. He learned to love God's voice and was quick to obey. He walked in the fullness of what he heard. Doing this enabled him to have an increasingly deep relationship with God. The biblical record shows he did so without compromise. His influence was enormous and all were aware of his favor with God. This allowed him to respond to the Spirit without self-made restraints or limits. Think about this - God wants to speak to you even more than you want to hear Him. Are you listening?

Stephen's Example in the face of his Martyrdom

Acts 7:55-58a, 59-60 (NLT)

"But Stephen, full of the Holy Spirit, gazed steadily upward into heaven and saw the glory of God, and he saw Jesus standing in the place of honor at God's right hand. {56} And he told them, "Look, I see the heavens opened and the Son of Man standing in the place of honor at God's right hand!" {57} Then they put their hands over their ears, and drowning out his voice with their shouts, they rushed at him. {58} They dragged him out of the city and began to stone him... {59} And as they stoned him, Stephen prayed, "Lord Jesus, receive my spirit." {60} And he fell to his knees, shouting, "Lord, don't charge them with this sin!" And with that, he died."

Stephen walked in such fullness of the Holy Spirit that, as he was being murdered, he was shown the glorified Lord Jesus, standing next to the Father in heaven. In that moment of death, Stephen demonstrated intimate, unusual access to God. His access was unrestricted by his circumstances. It was not limited by fear of death or any other emotion. His testimony would be eternal. In the fullness of the Holy Spirit, at that moment of his stoning, Stephen's face shone with glory. When his murderers looked upon him, they saw, in his face, a reflection of Jesus. Steven had become so much like Jesus that he even asked the Lord to forgive his murderers, just as Jesus had done when He was crucified.

Luke 23:33-34 (NKJV)

"And when they had come to the place called Calvary, there they crucified Him, and the criminals, one on the right hand and the other on the left. {34} Then Jesus said, "Father, forgive them, for they do not know what they do." And they divided His garments and cast lots."

Paul and Silas in the Philippian Jail

In Philippi, Paul had cast a demon out of a slave girl who was possessed by a spirit of divination. She told fortunes to make her masters money. Once freed from the evil spirit, she could no longer do this. Therefore, her masters seized Paul and Silas, dragged them into the marketplace, had them beaten and thrown into jail. Acts 16:16-26 recorded this series of events. As you read these Scriptures, you will find Paul and Silas praying and singing hymns to God. In the midst of their miserable situation, they were having sweet fellowship with the Lord. The response to their fellowship came from heaven. Their chains were broken and the prison doors were flung open by an earthquake. They gave evidence, through their worship, that continuous access to God destroyed the limits and chains of their circumstances. It will do the same for us.

Acts 16:22-26 (NKJV)

"Then the multitude rose up together against them; and the magistrates tore off their clothes and commanded them to be beaten with rods. {23} And when they had laid many stripes on them, they threw them into prison, commanding the jailer to keep them securely. {24} Having received such a charge, he put them into the inner prison and fastened their feet in the stocks. {25} But at midnight Paul and Silas were praying and singing hymns to God, and the prisoners were listening to them. {26} Suddenly there was a great earthquake, so that the foundations of the prison were shaken; and immediately all the doors were opened and everyone's chains were loosed."

Paul and Silas sang to the Lord in their chains. Their worship became a living demonstration of their unrestricted, unlimited and eternal fellowship with the Holy Spirit. Their circumstances said they could not get up and walk away from their chains. God said they could. He reacted to their demonstration of worship, and these men who could not get up and walk, did exactly that. They walked out of their chains. They walked out of their prison. They walked into their freedom. They did all of this in the fullness of the Holy Spirit. In what was the worst of situations, Paul and Silas maintained their access to Him. He honored their demonstration of this with His faithful, liberating response. Worship is a demonstration that breaks chains and opens prison doors. It enables access to the grace of God.

What can we learn about access to the fullness of the Holy Spirit from the examples of these four men of God?

1. Samuel heard the voice of God and drew close. As he grew, Samuel learned to enter more deeply into the access God had granted him. As a result, he continually walked in God's favor. The Holy Spirit was Samuel's spiritual walking companion throughout his life. His life was a demonstration of this.

2. Stephen's demonstration of his relationship with the Holy Spirit enabled him to face the worst imaginable circumstance. It carried him beyond the horrors of being stoned by hate-filled men. As the stones fell upon him, he walked in the fullness of the Holy Spirit, straight into the loving arms of Jesus.

3. Paul and Silas understood that their access to God could not be prevented by natural circumstances. They looked beyond the chains, even while wrapped in them. They chose to demonstrate their access through their worship and praise of God. Their decision to do this set heaven in motion. The jail was shaken. The chains were broken. Then, they walked out of their captivity into the arms of a grateful jailer. It was a walk in the fullness of the Holy Spirit.

As you can see, walking in the fullness of the Holy Spirit is a liberating journey. It provides us with an unrestricted, unlimited, eternal perspective on the reality of our blessings. We have been adopted by God as His sons and daughters. We get to be living demonstrations of this. We can have constant, unrestricted, unlimited and eternal access to the Father, Son and Holy Spirit!

Ephesians 2:16-18 (NIV)

"and in this one body to reconcile both of them to God through the cross, by which he put to death their hostility. {17} He came and preached peace to you who were far away and peace to those who were near. {18} For through him we both have access to the Father by one Spirit."

Questions for Discussion

1. Why is constant access to the Holy Spirit important enough to do anything necessary to obtain it - regardless of what changes it might demand from you?

2. Your continuous access to the Holy Spirit will provide that fullness in Him. The level of your influence among people will be enhanced greatly. Define what "influence" is and why it is important that you have it?

3. Why do you think people have so much trouble listening for the voice of the Holy Spirit? Do you think circumstances are the principle reason for this? Do you think habits and lifelong patterns are the reason? Perhaps you have another reason. If so, comment on this.

4. What would keep you from allowing what you have read in this chapter to change your life?

THREE

The Power of Constant Access
(Unrestrained, Unlimited and Endless)

Acts 1:4-5 (NKJV)

"And being assembled together with them, He commanded them not to depart from Jerusalem, but to wait for the Promise of the Father, "which," He said, "you have heard from Me; {5} for John truly baptized with water, but you shall be baptized with the Holy Spirit not many days from now.""

Acts 1:8 (NKJV)

"But you shall receive power when the Holy Spirit has come upon you; and you shall be witnesses to Me in Jerusalem, and in all Judea and Samaria, and to the end of the earth."

In Acts 1:4-8, Jesus promised us power. He made this promise just before He was taken up in a cloud to the Father. Let's unpack Verses 5 and 8 to begin to understand Christ's promise of power.

1. In Verse 5, Jesus announced the coming baptism in the Holy Spirit. This was to be a door to the fullness of

God's power, and it was. Today, we should welcome it as an open door to great potential for our spiritual growth. Then, we ought to do our best to walk in the fullness we have received, making it a reality in our lives.

2. In Verse 8, Jesus revealed that power is sourced supernaturally when the Holy Spirit has *"come upon"* us. The result will be that we have within us, the potential to see His power come alive in and through us.

When Jesus announced that the power of the Holy Spirit was to come at Pentecost, He knew that having this power would be conditional. It would depend upon our willingness to receive the promise and demonstrate it through our faith and obedience. Having God's power begins by believing that God is who He says He is and will do what He says He will do.

In Acts, Chapter 2, the promise of power was manifested. This power was the fulfillment of God's earlier promise recorded in Joel 2:28-32. Many Christians (and perhaps most of us) do not walk in God's power, and especially in its fullness. Why is this?

Degrees of Power

Luke 3:16 (NKJV)

"John answered, saying to all, "I indeed baptize you with water; but One mightier than I is coming, whose sandal strap I am not worthy to loose. He will baptize you with the Holy Spirit and fire."

Degrees of faith determine degrees of power. This is a cause and effect principle.

Power	
Cause	Effect
No Faith	No Power
Low Levels of Faith	Low Power
Normal Levels of Faith	Average, Everyday Power
High Levels of Faith	Great Power Faith, obedience and love all work together to produce power.
Holy Spirit-Filled Faith (Baptized with Fire)	Unrestrained, Unlimited, Endless Power This is a condition in which our potential to walk in the fullness of the power of Holy Spirit is reached.

Let's look again at the biblical examples of Samuel, Stephen and Paul, who operated in the fullness of their faith and saw God's power manifest in their lives. Their examples are very different, but all of them share the same divine power source. They were full of high or even unrestrained, unlimited power. The power manifested, depending on the circumstances at the moment of their need or opportunity. It was always the power of the Holy Spirit that moved through them.

Samuel: Full of Holy Spirit Power

In the previous chapter, we saw that the Prophet Samuel had been close to God. He had experienced continuous access to God's voice since he was a small child. Because of this access, Samuel was able to operate powerfully in his gift of prophecy. Whenever he spoke for God, it was a demonstration of his faith-filled commitment to God. The Holy Spirit responded to this commitment by putting God's power-filled message in Samuel's mouth. Samuel was God's covenant enforcer of his day. When he spoke, people fully expected his words to be followed by God's actions to confirm what he said. They respected and feared Samuel's words because they carried God's power.

An example of the fullness of the Holy Spirit's power in Samuel's words occurred following King Saul's disobedience of Samuel's prophetic instructions. Contrary to these instructions, after Saul's victory at the city of Amalek, Saul spared King Agag and preserved the best of Agag's goods and animals. Then, instead of waiting for Samuel, as he had been told, Saul sacrificed to the Lord before Samuel arrived. Saul's disobedience would cost him the destiny that he could have enjoyed. The Scriptures show us Samuel's response to Saul's disobedience.

1 Samuel 15:14-19, 22-23 (NKJV)

"But Samuel said, "What then is this bleating of the sheep in my ears, and the lowing of the oxen which I hear?" {15} And Saul said, "They have brought them from the Amalekites; for the people

30

spared the best of the sheep and the oxen, to sacrifice to the LORD your God; and the rest we have utterly destroyed." {16} Then Samuel said to Saul, "Be quiet! And I will tell you what the LORD said to me last night." And he said to him, "Speak on." {17} So Samuel said, "When you were little in your own eyes, were you not head of the tribes of Israel? And did not the LORD anoint you king over Israel? {18} Now the LORD sent you on a mission, and said, 'Go, and utterly destroy the sinners, the Amalekites, and fight against them until they are consumed.' {19} Why then did you not obey the voice of the LORD? Why did you swoop down on the spoil, and do evil in the sight of the LORD?... {22} "Then Samuel said: "Has the LORD as great delight in burnt offerings and sacrifices, As in obeying the voice of the LORD? Behold, to obey is better than sacrifice, And to heed than the fat of rams. {23} For rebellion is as the sin of witchcraft, And stubbornness is as iniquity and idolatry. Because you have rejected the word of the LORD, He also has rejected you from being king.""

Samuel's prophetic declaration that the Lord had rejected Saul as king had the full weight and power of God. Saul tried to seek Samuel's pardon and blessing. He could not get it, and Samuel told him why. As Samuel spoke, the power of God filled his words. Therefore, Saul had no choice. He accepted the prophetic words. He was tormented from that time forward until his death. This narrative teaches that

31

when you have an intimate relationship with God, the words you speak will have the potential to be infinite in power.

Stephen: Full Faith and Power

We have seen that at the end of Stephen's life, he was full of faith and access to the Holy Spirit. Acts 6:5 shows us he was like that from the beginning of his walk with God.

Acts 6:1-6 (NLT)

"But as the believers rapidly multiplied, there were rumblings of discontent. Those who spoke Greek complained against those who spoke Hebrew, saying that their widows were being discriminated against in the daily distribution of food. {2} So the Twelve called a meeting of all the believers. "We apostles should spend our time preaching and teaching the word of God, not administering a food program," they said. {3} "Now look around among yourselves, friends, and select seven men who are well respected and are full of the Holy Spirit and wisdom. We will put them in charge of this business. {4} Then we can spend our time in prayer and preaching and teaching the word." {5} This idea pleased the whole group, and they chose the following: Stephen (a man full of faith and the Holy Spirit), Philip, Procorus, Nicanor, Timon, Parmenas, and Nicolas of Antioch (a Gentile convert to the Jewish faith, who had now become a Christian). {6} These seven were presented to the apostles,

who prayed for them as they laid their hands on them."

The power of the Holy Spirit was so strong in Stephen that he could stand, proclaiming the Gospel, in the face of violent enemies of the Lord. He rebuked them, knowing it would lead him to a horrific stoning and death. His power was not only to endure the torture and death, but also to deliver the word of the Lord with authority and truth.

Acts 7:51-53 (NKJV)

"You stiffnecked and uncircumcised in heart and ears! You always resist the Holy Spirit; as your fathers did, so do you. {52} Which of the prophets did your fathers not persecute? And they killed those who foretold the coming of the Just One, of whom you now have become the betrayers and murderers, {53} who have received the law by the direction of angels and have not kept it."

When you have an intimate relationship with the Holy Spirit, you will see far beyond the circumstances of the moment. You will not be alone. You will see Jesus.

Paul and Silas: Full Faith and Power

We saw that, while in Philippi, Paul and Silas had cast a demon out of a slave girl who was possessed by a spirit of divination. Let's look at this same account, now taking note of the authority in which Paul and Silas walked.

33

When the demon possessed slave girl began to follow Paul and Silas to mock their ministry, they were completely filled with faith and power to overcome the demon. It was there to distract them and stop them from their mission. It had no ability to do this against Paul and Silas, because they were full of God's power.

Acts 16:16-18a (NKJV)

"Now it happened, as we went to prayer, that a certain slave girl possessed with a spirit of divination met us, who brought her masters much profit by fortune-telling. {17} This girl followed Paul and us, and cried out, saying, "These men are the servants of the Most High God, who proclaim to us the way of salvation." {18} And this she did for many days. But Paul, greatly annoyed, turned and said to the spirit, "I command you in the name of Jesus Christ to come out of her." And he came out that very hour. {19} But when her masters saw that their hope of profit was gone, they seized Paul and Silas and dragged them into the marketplace to the authorities."

The Greek word in Verse 17 that is translated *"cried out"* is *"krazo,"*[4] (pronounced "krad'-zo.") It implies making a loud croaking sound like a frog or a shriek like a wild animal in the forest. You can imagine how disruptive and distracting the demon in that slave girl must have been. Whenever Paul and Silas began to preach about Jesus, the shrieking demon-possessed girl would disrupt their message. It was an

---

[4] Strong's Number G2896.

34

assignment from hell that had to be broken. Paul took authority over the demon in the name of Jesus, and it came out. Paul and Simon were seized and beaten. Then they were imprisoned in a dark, inner part of the jail. The fullness of their faith and power in the Holy Spirit would sustain them. God had a plan for them. Their chains were part of it. The plan would be accomplished through their imprisonment, chains and miraculous release. Their jailer and his family were redeemed and brought into God's kingdom.

Paul and Silas had come to Philippi, walking in the fullness of the Holy Spirit. Their ministry reflected the fullness of their spiritual authority. They fulfilled the will of God wherever they went and people were set free in Christ. Rely on the fullness of your faith and power. It will take others out of their personal prisons. (It might even deliver you from yours.)

We can learn so much about the full faith and power in the Holy Spirit that we have seen from the examples of these four men of God.
- Samuel, whose prophetic voice was filled with power
- Stephen, who displayed fiery zeal for the Lord and fearlessness in the face of imminent, horrific death
- Paul and Silas, who walked in faith and power through every difficulty and never wavered

Questions for Discussion

1. Why was Samuel so upset with King Saul when Saul sacrificed to the Lord without Samuel being there?

2. How do Stephen's words to his killers demonstrate unrestricted, unlimited power to you? Explain in detail.

3. Why does God allow us to be persecuted, as Paul and Silas were, so that His will can be fulfilled?

FOUR

Fire from Heaven
(Unrestrained, Unlimited and Endless)

Both the Old and New Testaments provide numerous accounts of the demonstration of God's power. In this chapter, we will continue this important subject; and, see how God manifests or projects His power both sovereignly and by a visible demonstration through his servants.

Acts 2:1-4 (NKJV)

"When the Day of Pentecost had fully come, they were all with one accord in one place. {2} And suddenly there came a sound from heaven, as of a rushing mighty wind, and it filled the whole house where they were sitting. {3} Then there appeared to them divided tongues, as of fire, and one sat upon each of them. {4} And they were all filled with the Holy Spirit and began to speak with other tongues, as the Spirit gave them utterance."

Fire was a biblical sign of divine power. On the Day of Pentecost, God chose to send down a sovereign, visible demonstration of this power. The events of Pentecost left no doubt that the fire came from heaven. The *"tongues, as of fire"* were supernatural in origin. They clearly came from the Holy Spirit. Many of those present that day were familiar with the Hebrew Scriptures. This demonstration must surely have reminded them of events such as the provision of the pillar of fire that guided the Israelites through the desert. It was also reminiscent of the Prophet Elijah's call to God for fire to consume the sacrifice on the altar, in his confrontation with the prophets of Baal. In this chapter, we will look at Elijah's sacrificial altar and the response of fire from God. Then we will continue by looking at God's people in the New Testament, who received that fire and subsequently, walked in its fullness.

An Old Testament Demonstration

Elijah had a fiery jealousy and zeal for God. He faithfully nurtured this fire in his heart. It led to an extraordinary anointing for power. Everyone, including his enemies, came to know that Elijah walked so closely to the Holy Spirit that he was not to be opposed. The prophets of Baal found this out. On an altar of fire, came a demonstration by Elijah of his unrestrained, unlimited, constant access to the power of the Holy Spirit. Elijah was not playing a guessing-game with that water-soaked altar. He was not merely hoping for a fiery miracle. He knew that the level of his access to the Holy Spirit's power was so high that he could ask for fire from heaven and God would provide it. Here is the biblical narrative:

1 Kings 18:22-24 (NKJV)

"Then Elijah said to the people, "I alone am left a prophet of the LORD; but Baal's prophets are four hundred and fifty men. {23} Therefore let

38

them give us two bulls; and let them choose one bull for themselves, cut it in pieces, and lay it on the wood, but put no fire under it; and I will prepare the other bull, and lay it on the wood, but put no fire under it. Then you call on the name of your gods, and I will call on the name of the LORD; and the God who answers by fire, He is God." So all the people answered and said, "It is well spoken.""

1 Kings 18:36-39 (NKJV)

"And it came to pass, at the time of the offering of the evening sacrifice, that Elijah the prophet came near and said, "LORD God of Abraham, Isaac, and Israel, let it be known this day that You are God in Israel and I am Your servant, and that I have done all these things at Your word. {37} Hear me, O LORD, hear me, that this people may know that You are the LORD God, and that You have turned their hearts back to You again." {38} Then the fire of the LORD fell and consumed the burnt sacrifice, and the wood and the stones and the dust, and it licked up the water that was in the trench. {39} Now when all the people saw it, they fell on their faces; and they said, "The LORD, He is God! The LORD, He is God!""

Elijah's encounter with the prophets of Baal teaches that the greatest demonstration of your access to the power of the Holy Spirit will be when your prayers cause others to proclaim, *"The LORD, He is God!"* When you demonstrate

39

your faith in God, You will see God faithfully respond to you... with power!

A New Testament Demonstration

In Acts, Chapter 2, Peter responded to the tongues of fire at Pentecost by preaching with great boldness. This was the first of many demonstrations of the power in which he now walked. Chapter 3 recorded Peter and John walking toward the temple. They encountered a man who had never walked. He was carried every day to the gate of the temple to beg. He asked them for some money. Peter's response was a demonstration of compassionate power. He called down a creative healing miracle from heaven.

Acts 3:6-10 (NKJV)

"Then Peter said, "Silver and gold I do not have, but what I do have I give you: In the name of Jesus Christ of Nazareth, rise up and walk." {7} And he took him by the right hand and lifted him up, and immediately his feet and ankle bones received strength. {8} So he, leaping up, stood and walked and entered the temple with them; walking, leaping, and praising God. {9} And all the people saw him walking and praising God. {10} Then they knew that it was he who sat begging alms at the Beautiful Gate of the temple; and they were filled with wonder and amazement at what had happened to him."

This miracle narrative teaches us the following about how we are to demonstrate the power of God.

40

1. Be sure to demonstrate God's power by calling on the name of Jesus. Do this with fiery faith in His name.

2. Do not let what seem to be impossible circumstances cause you to hesitate or lose faith.

3. Be bold. Do whatever the Holy Spirit tells you to do. Do it immediately. Do it with fiery zeal!

4. It will not be necessary to justify your boldness or explain what God has done. Everyone will know. Use the miracle to draw people near so you can preach the Gospel.

5. All glory goes to the Lord Jesus Christ. Do not let your emotions convince you to take any of His glory. Be humble. Be thankful. Be glad someone was healed.

The Fullness of Grace and Power

Acts 6:8 (NIV)

"Now Stephen, a man full of God's grace and power, did great wonders and miraculous signs among the people."

This verse describes Stephen as someone whose daily life demonstrated a fullness of faith in Christ and the fullness of power in the Holy Spirit. His ministry must have been amazing, as he attracted the attention of those who were at enmity with the church. Christ's enemies would have feared the miracles and signs, because these miracles would have drawn many to accept Christ and receive their salvation. As a result of this (as we learned in the previous chapter), the religious, hard-hearted men of the temple were compelled to stone Stephen to death. This ended Stephen's ministry among them, but could not stop the effect of what he had demonstrated. His ministry remains in the record of the Scriptures forever. It still ministers to us today.

Overflowing with Power

Acts 9:1-6 (NKJV)

"Then Saul, still breathing threats and murder against the disciples of the Lord, went to the high priest {2} and asked letters from him to the synagogues of Damascus, so that if he found any who were of the Way, whether men or women, he might bring them bound to Jerusalem. {3} As he journeyed he came near Damascus, and suddenly a light shone around him from heaven. {4} Then he fell to the ground, and heard a voice saying to him, "Saul, Saul, why are you persecuting Me?" {5} And he said, "Who are You, Lord?" Then the Lord said, "I am Jesus, whom you are persecuting. It is hard for you to kick against the goads." {6} So he, trembling and astonished, said, "Lord, what do You want me to do?" Then the Lord said to him, "Arise and go into the city, and you will be told what you must do.""

Everything about Saul of Tarsus was anti-Christ until he met Christ Himself. Saul was traveling on the road to Damascus. His assignment, authorized by the religious authorities, was to persecute Christians. In an instant, Jesus freed him of this demonic assignment. He gave Saul a new assignment. Now Saul would destroy the works of the very same demons he used to walk with and serve. His service from that moment forward would be for God. He would do so, walking in the fullness of the Holy Spirit. This was Saul's destiny. It came from the highest authority in heaven. It came through the power of the Holy Spirit. Saul was transformed into a new man. Now, he would be the Apostle Paul.

Acts 19:11-12 (NLT)

"God gave Paul the power to do unusual miracles, {12} so that even when handkerchiefs or cloths that had touched his skin were placed on sick people, they were healed of their diseases, and any evil spirits within them came out."

Paul would walk in what was arguably the most powerful anointing a man can have. This was the anointing to *"do unusual miracles."* (I am not sure I can define an unusual miracle, except to say that it was far beyond anyone's expectations or understanding, even for miracles.) Everyday objects like handkerchiefs and napkins carried Paul's anointing for these *"unusual miracles."* These objects overflowed with the Holy Spirit's power, simply because Paul had touched them. When these objects came in physical contact with people, or even just came into close proximity, the healing anointing was transferred from them. As this happened, demons were terrorized and fled. Sickness immediately had its assignment canceled. Ordinary objects became extraordinary demonstrations of the fullness of the power of the Holy Spirit.

We can learn from Paul's example. If you want to walk in the fullness of the Holy Spirit, demonstrating His majestic omnipotence throughout your life, submit to the following:

1. Make it your constant practice to ask, *"Lord, what do you want me to do?"* (Acts 9:6)

2. Believe God without doubt or wavering, regardless of natural circumstances. Behave according to what you believe. Then expect nothing less than a miracle.

3. Learn to love God's Word. Devour it daily. Have a hunger for the Bible that cannot be satisfied.

4. Learn to love the people who can benefit from your willingness to work *"unusual miracles."* God's love is the power behind the anointing for miracles, and certainly, what may be called unusual ones. Miracles happen because *"God is love."* This means that Jesus is love. The Father is love. The Holy Spirit is love. The power that springs from their love knows no limits. It cannot be contained.

1 John 4:16 (NKJV)

"And we have known and believed the love that God has for us. God is love, and he who abides in love abides in God, and God in him."

The Power Team: Paul and Silas

Acts 16:16-18 (NKJV)

"Now it happened, as we went to prayer, that a certain slave girl possessed with a spirit of

divination met us, who brought her masters much profit by fortune-telling. {17} This girl followed Paul and us, and cried out, saying, "These men are the servants of the Most High God, who proclaim to us the way of salvation." {18} And this she did for many days. But Paul, greatly annoyed, turned and said to the spirit, "I command you in the name of Jesus Christ to come out of her." And he came out that very hour."

The original Greek word translated *"that very hour"* by the NKJV, or *"instantly"* by the NLT is *"hora."*[5] This is a prime Greek word. It defines Paul's deliverance of the slave girl as an instantaneous occurrence. That is how quickly a demon obeys, when the person exercising God's authority is walking in the constant fullness of the Holy Spirit.

When Paul spoke to cast out the demon, it was not a suggestion, a plea or an expression of hope. It was purely a demonstration. Paul was on assignment from God. He and Silas walked in the deep fullness of their relationship with the Holy Spirit. This made the fullness of God's power available for Paul to demonstrate. The demon in the slave girl had no choice. It could not argue, hesitate or try to remain entrenched within her. It had to bow to the name of Jesus and go.[6] It could not even think of challenging Paul's command. The slave girl was freed *"instantly."*

---

[5] Strong's Number G5610.
[6] See also, Philippians 2:8-11.

A Final Reminder (and Warning)

Zechariah 4:6-7 (NKJV)

"So he answered and said to me: "This is the word of the LORD to Zerubbabel: 'Not by might nor by power, but by My Spirit,' Says the LORD of hosts. {7} 'Who are you, O great mountain? Before Zerubbabel you shall become a plain! And he shall bring forth the capstone With shouts of "Grace, grace to it!"'"

About twenty-five hundred years ago, an angel was sent by God to speak these words to the Prophet Zechariah. They are an appropriate warning and a key encouragement for success in our power ministries. We are to give God glory continually for the miracles we experience. We are not to fall into the trap of thinking the things we demonstrate for the Lord are signs to point toward us. They are signs pointing to Christ alone. It is His power, at work through us, accessed in the fullness of the Holy Spirit.

No Access	= No Power
Low Access	= Low Power
Some Access	= Some Power
Full Access	= Fullness of Power

The quality of your power in the Holy Spirit will depend upon your choices. Which of the four levels of access will you choose? Before you answer, be sure to measure the cost in terms of personal commitment.

Questions for Discussion

1. How would you define fiery faith?

2. What would you say to people who tell you they do not believe in demons? This is often a difficult question to answer. (If you do not believe in demons, I would encourage you to study what the Scriptures teach about this subject, and then make your own judgment.)

3. What would you do if someone asked you to pray for a person who seemed to have a demon? (This is also not an easy question to answer.)

4. Zechariah 4:7 speaks of mountain-moving faith. What do you think is the key to anyone having mountain moving faith?

FIVE

Wisdom from God
(Unrestrained, Unlimited and Endless)

Solomon

King Solomon walked in the fullness of God-given wisdom and understanding, surpassing all others. He was the wisest man who ever lived.

1 Kings 3:5, 8-9, 12 (NKJV)

"At Gibeon the LORD appeared to Solomon in a dream by night; and God said, "Ask! What shall I give you?""

SOLOMON:
{8} "And Your servant is in the midst of Your people whom You have chosen, a great people, too numerous to be numbered or counted. {9} Therefore give to Your servant an understanding heart to judge Your people, that I may discern between good and evil. For who is able to judge this great people of Yours."

THE LORD:
{12} "behold, I have done according to your words; see, I have given you a wise and

understanding heart, so that there has not been anyone like you before you, nor shall any like you arise after you.""

God invited Solomon to ask for anything. Solomon could have asked for riches, power, long life or anything else. Instead, he asked for *"an understanding heart."* God gave Solomon what he asked for. He provided Solomon with access to unrestrained, unlimited wisdom and understanding. In the beginnings of Solomon's reign, he exercised wisdom without equal. He demonstrated how special this gift was, and the results blessed his kingdom.

Unfortunately for Solomon, he became blind to the value of the wisdom and understanding he had been given. He stopped being obedient to God and His Word. He turned from God. He turned to idol worship. He spent much of his life in the foolishness of self-gratification and the disobedience of prideful living. Solomon wasted this precious gift of wisdom on sinful living. The results were tragic. Take every opportunity to ask God for what you need that will enable you to make a difference for others. Then, when the Lord provides it, be sure to use it wisely. Do not waste what God has blessed you with.

A Prayer for Spiritual Wisdom and Understanding

Ephesians 1:16-20 (NLT)

"I have never stopped thanking God for you. I pray for you constantly, {17} asking God, the glorious Father of our Lord Jesus Christ, to give you spiritual wisdom and understanding, so that

you might grow in your knowledge of God. {18} I pray that your hearts will be flooded with light so that you can understand the wonderful future he has promised to those he called. I want you to realize what a rich and glorious inheritance he has given to his people. {19} I pray that you will begin to understand the incredible greatness of his power for us who believe him. This is the same mighty power {20} that raised Christ from the dead and seated him in the place of honor at God's right hand in the heavenly realms..."

Let's unpack this prayer. The purpose of doing so is to bring clarity and understanding about the benefits of wisdom that come with walking in the fullness of the Holy Spirit. Here are three key points to consider.

Key Point One - Spiritual Wisdom and Understanding

Ephesians 1:17 (NLT)

"...asking God, the glorious Father of our Lord Jesus Christ, to give you spiritual wisdom and understanding, so that you might grow in your knowledge of God."

Paul prays that his readers would achieve the goal of spiritual wisdom and understanding that comes from the Father. It will result in growing in the knowledge of God.

1. Paul knew the value of walking in spiritual wisdom and understanding. He was fully aware that its characteristics

51

are unique and different from those of natural wisdom and understanding. Accordingly, Paul prayed for the Father to provide the Ephesians (and subsequently all believers) with supernaturally sourced wisdom.

John 16:13-15 (NKJV)

"However, when He, the Spirit of truth, has come, He will guide you into all truth; for He will not speak on His own authority, but whatever He hears He will speak; and He will tell you things to come. {14} He will glorify Me, for He will take of what is Mine and declare it to you. {15} All things that the Father has are Mine. Therefore I said that He will take of Mine and declare it to you."

2. As our heavenly Father gives us this supernaturally sourced wisdom, we are able to use it in partnership with, and by the direction of the Holy Spirit.

3. Without the Holy Spirit's direction, we cannot properly apply spiritual wisdom and understanding. There will be neither ability nor opportunity to walk in the fullness of the Holy Spirit. We will have only our imperfect, natural wisdom and understanding upon which to rely.

Spiritual wisdom and understanding are effective tools. Sharpen them in your prayer and devotional time with God.

Key Point Two - Illumination

Ephesians 1:18 (NLT)

"I pray that your hearts will be flooded with light so that you can understand the wonderful

future he has promised to those he called. I want you to realize what a rich and glorious inheritance he has given to his people."

As our hearts are illuminated with the truth, we will understand the bright future God has for us. Verse 18, in the New Living Translation (NLT), informs us that Paul prayed for our hearts to be *"flooded with light."* This leads us to ask, "What is this light?" 1 John 1:5 clearly answered this question at its purest, foundational level.

1 John 1:5 (NKJV)

"This is the message which we have heard from Him and declare to you, that God is light and in Him is no darkness at all."

By studying Ephesians 1:18 and 1 John 1:5 together, we may conclude the following:

1. Paul prayed for illumination, or that we would be *"flooded with light"* (flooded with God) in our hearts. Specifically, Paul asked that our understanding of what we see, hear and know, would be *"enlightened"* (NKJV) by God's presence, as He works through the fullness of His Spirit in us.

2. Paul's prayer made clear that the hope of God's calling is within each of us to see. It will show us a clear picture of what the Lord has promised. Apply His wisdom to your hopes and you will see them realized.

3. We have an inheritance, through God, awaiting us. The inheritance, about which Paul wrote, is bright with God's

53

presence and rich in His glory. It is in His hands right now! It waits for the time when our hopes become reality. Then, we will see it clearly, because our heavenly Father is called *"Abba."* (This is an ancient expression of endearment that a child would call his or her father.)

Romans 8:14-17a (NKJV)

"For as many as are led by the Spirit of God, these are sons of God. {15} For you did not receive the spirit of bondage again to fear, but you received the Spirit of adoption by whom we cry out, "Abba, Father." {16} The Spirit Himself bears witness with our spirit that we are children of God, {17} and if children, then heirs; heirs of God and joint heirs with Christ..."

Romans 8:15 established that we are our heavenly Father's children by adoption. This is a legal term. We are legally His heirs and joint heirs with His Son, Jesus. Do not deny yourself your inheritance because you lack faith, fail to be obedient, or neglect to claim it. Wisdom says, receive your adoption as His gift and walk in its fullness.

Supernaturally sourced wisdom is part of our inheritance. Be wise and understanding about your rights and privileges as a child of God. Accept them, and guard the responsibilities that go with them.

Look to the Holy Spirit for the wisdom that only comes from Him. It will take you securely to your hopes. It is fully attainable as you walk wisely in the fullness of His Spirit.

54

Key Point Three - Power

Ephesians 1:19-20 (NLT)

"I pray that you will begin to understand the incredible greatness of his power for us who believe him. This is the same mighty power {20} that raised Christ from the dead and seated him in the place of honor at God's right hand in the heavenly realms."

Wisdom from God is power. God has great power awaiting those who believe. As children of God, we must be willing to carry out the responsibilities that this includes. We must not settle for less than the fullness of this power.

1. Understanding the power inherent in godly wisdom liberates the child of God from limitations. The Holy Spirit delivers this power to us through revelation of the truth. Then, the truth sets us free and keeps us free. Freedom in Christ is our inherent right, as adopted sons and daughters of God.

2. The thankful, careful application of God's wisdom positions us to experience God-pleasing success in our lives. As this happens, we are able to understand the power in removing what would not please God from our ways of living and embracing what would please Him. We will progress towards being fully pleasing to Him, walking in the fullness of the Holy Spirit. This sequence describes the process of sanctification. Paul desired that we would become sanctified, or that we would mature in Christ. He knew we could have the unrestrained,

unlimited, endless ability to grow in Christ and please the Father. Paul encouraged us to make this our aim, in every circumstance. It was his desire and his prayer.

2 Corinthians 5:9 (NKJV)

"Therefore we make it our aim, whether present or absent, to be well pleasing to Him."

Colossians 1:9-10 (NKJV)

"For this reason we also, since the day we heard it, do not cease to pray for you, and to ask that you may be filled with the knowledge of His will in all wisdom and spiritual understanding; {10} that you may walk worthy of the Lord, fully pleasing Him, being fruitful in every good work and increasing in the knowledge of God;"

Questions for Discussion

1. How would you define the term *"power?"*

2. How does more of God's wisdom and understanding in you make you free of things that have limited you?

3. What limitations could most Christians overcome by having more of God's wisdom and understanding?

SIX

Guarding Your Access to God's Wisdom

As we did in the previous chapter, let's begin with the exchange between the LORD and King Solomon.

The Wisdom of Solomon

1 Kings 3:5, 9a, 12 (NKJV)

"At Gibeon the LORD appeared to Solomon in a dream by night; and God said, "Ask! What shall I give you?""

<u>Solomon:</u>
{9} "Therefore give to Your servant an understanding heart to judge Your people, that I may discern between good and evil...."

<u>The LORD:</u>
{12}"behold, I have done according to your words; see, I have given you a wise and understanding heart..."

Solomon's *"understanding heart"* was a heart with full access to God's wisdom. You can see this in the way Solomon judged between two women who claimed to be mother of the same child. Below, is the narrative of

Solomon's decision, following the women's conflicting claims for the living child.

1 Kings 3:23-28 (NKJV)

"And the king said, "The one says, 'This is my son, who lives, and your son is the dead one'; and the other says, 'No! But your son is the dead one, and my son is the living one.'" {24} Then the king said, "Bring me a sword." So they brought a sword before the king. {25} And the king said, "Divide the living child in two, and give half to one, and half to the other." {26} Then the woman whose son was living spoke to the king, for she yearned with compassion for her son; and she said, "O my lord, give her the living child, and by no means kill him!" But the other said, "Let him be neither mine nor yours, but divide him." {27} So the king answered and said, "Give the first woman the living child, and by no means kill him; she is his mother.' {28} And all Israel heard of the judgment which the king had rendered; and they feared the king for they saw that... the wisdom of God was in him to administer justice."

The connection between Solomon's request for *"an understanding heart"* and the wise judgment he made reveals a key aspect of walking in the fullness of the Holy Spirit, which is great success. As long as Solomon conducted himself with the wisdom of God, he was successful. The people for whom he was responsible were safe and prosperous. Solomon made a difference in the quality of their lives. We know that later in life he lost his way and turned from serving God. When this happened, people could no longer say of him, *"the wisdom of God was in him to administer justice."* Solomon traded his position of having access to wisdom and favor with the Lord for that of a common fool. The results were tragic for God's people, and especially for Solomon's own family.

You must safeguard your access to the wisdom of God. To continue to hear from God and be an influence to those around you, here are four things you can do:

1. Stay humble and make the fear of the Lord your lifetime safety zone in all that you decide to do.

    In his later years, Solomon reflected on the foolishness of his own life. Would he have remembered the following proverb he had written, with great regret? It is the perfect picture of the contrast between how high Solomon started and how low the pit was into which he took himself.

    Proverbs 1:7 (NKJV)

    "The fear of the LORD is the beginning of knowledge... But fools despise wisdom and instruction."

2. Be diligent to learn and apply the wisdom you find in the Word of God. This will assure you of God's favor and blessings; and, you will fulfill your life's journey before Him to its fullest. Diligence might even get you to the place in God where you can receive wisdom in all its fullness. (Diligence means you approach a task with a

59

meticulous, thorough and careful attitude. You do your best and complete it with excellence.)

2 Timothy 2:15 (NKJV)

"Be diligent to present yourself approved to God, a worker who does not need to be ashamed, rightly dividing the word of truth."

3. Be led by the Spirit of God. This will require that you hear Him, in whatever way He speaks to you. For this to happen, you will need to form the habit of listening throughout the day. It will be especially vital to listen in the midst of important decisions you will make. Solomon practiced this in the beginnings of his reign, but later listened to other voices that led him into sin. Be sure you listen to the right voices and reject the wrong ones.

   One of my principles for championship Christian living is that "God's champions do not decide their futures. They decide their habits and their habits decide their futures." (Now would be a good time to pause and think about this principle. How can you apply it to yourself so that you keep the door open to God's wisdom?)

4. Determine to run your race faithfully all the way to the finish. This will keep you positioned for every victory and blessing that God has for you. The Apostle Paul understood this and never lost sight of it. He was a properly positioned finisher.

Philippians 3:13-15 (GWT)

"Brothers and sisters, I can't consider myself

a winner yet. This is what I do: I don't look back, I lengthen my stride, and {14} I run straight toward the goal to win the prize that God's heavenly call offers in Christ Jesus. {15} Whoever has a mature faith should think this way. And if you think differently, God will show you how to think."

Paul completely fulfilled the will of God for his life, which included having the gift of continued access to God's wisdom. He used this wisdom from the Holy Spirit to write one third of the New Testament.

Like Paul, we are called to fulfill the will of God. Pray for the wisdom that the Holy Spirit makes available to those who seek to serve, as Paul did. Ultimately, this wisdom is available to those who have an undivided heart for God, walk in mature faith and refuse to be denied their destinies.

Both Solomon's and Paul's inspired writings are sources of unusual, extraordinary wisdom. Nevertheless, the contrast between the outcomes of their lives provides a clear picture of the choices we have as children of God. Both men touched countless people through their written words. However, Solomon's ending led to tragedy and sorrow. Paul's ending led to triumph through the growth of the Gospel. His life demonstrated that constant wisdom and understanding can be yours when you follow the Word of God. Reject it and you should expect far less than God intended for you and perhaps even great personal loss.

The Wisdom of James

Acts, Chapter 15 records a dispute that arose among the early Christians at Antioch. The disagreement concerned whether a Gentile man must be circumcised to be saved. The church decided that Paul and Barnabus, along with some others, should be sent to Jerusalem to ask about this. When they arrived in Jerusalem, the apostles and elders gathered to discuss this question. This prompted Peter to give his testimony of what the Holy Spirit had done at Cornelius' house. Peter testified that God made it clear that there was no longer a difference between Jewish and Gentile believers. His experience at Cornelius' house confirmed that salvation through grace was for anyone, regardless of race, past religion or culture. Salvation was not dependent on works. For those gathered in Jerusalem, this was new. It certainly must have seemed unusual. Peter's words were wisdom straight from the Holy Spirit. For some, it would have been difficult to accept. (See Acts 15:7-11 and Ephesians 2:8-10).

James, the leading apostle, was a man filled with God's wisdom. He announced to the gathering how the dispute would be solved. He quoted from the Book of Amos.

Amos 9:11-12 (NKJV)

"On that day I will raise up The tabernacle of David, which has fallen down, And repair its damages; I will raise up its ruins, And rebuild it as in the days of old; {12} That they may possess the remnant of Edom, And all the Gentiles who are called by My name," Says the LORD who does this thing."

Using these Scriptures to validate his authority, he proceeded to provide the solution, which supported Peter's testimony that the door was open for Gentile salvation. He did this by using the wisdom the Holy Spirit had given him. His references to the Hebrew Scriptures, along with the boundaries he set, allowed the Jewish believers present that day to accept their Gentile brothers and sisters, without feeling they would have to reject their own culture. Here is the biblical account:

Acts 15:13-20 (NKJV)

"And after they had become silent, James answered, saying, "Men and brethren, listen to me: {14} Simon has declared how God at the first visited the Gentiles to take out of them a people for His name. {15} And with this the words of the prophets agree, just as it is written: {16} 'After this I will return And will rebuild the tabernacle of David, which has fallen down; I will rebuild its ruins, And I will set it up; {17} So that the rest of mankind may seek the LORD, Even all the Gentiles who are called by My name, Says the LORD who does all these things.' {18} Known to God from eternity are all His works. {19} Therefore I judge that we should not trouble those from among the Gentiles who are turning to God, {20} but that we write to them to abstain from things polluted by idols, from sexual immorality, from things strangled, and from blood."

In Acts 15:19-20, James announced his conclusion. It was a judgment of unusual, extraordinary wisdom from God. The Gentiles were not to be burdened with circumcision. They were only asked to abstain from idol worship. He reinforced this with specific instructions, which he broke into four categories:

1. Gentile Christian were to abstain from anything polluted by idols. (This would have included food, physical objects and cultural activities.)

2. There was to be no sexual immorality among them.

3. They could not eat anything that had been strangled.

4. They could not eat anything that was prepared while still containing blood, nor could they consume the blood itself.

These four issues, directly connected to idol worship, were offensive to God and therefore, a sin. James' declaration left most of the Gentile believers' everyday cultural activities intact. It also did not impose circumcision upon the Gentiles. The apostles and elders wrote of this decision in a letter and sent it to Antioch. When the Christians at Antioch read it, they *"rejoiced over its encouragement"* (Acts 16:31).

James showed his extraordinary God-given wisdom in selecting these four categories. His was an example of walking in the wisdom of God that we all should strive to have. James had unrestrained, unlimited access to the Lord's wisdom, and he used it. His decision removed tensions that could have brought disunity to the church. It became a standard for all Christians, then and now.

James' wrote of the contrast between earthly foolishness and sensuality, and God's kind of wisdom. Here is the comparison he presents in James, Chapter 3:

A Comparison of the Two Kinds of Wisdom From James 3:13-17 (NKJV)		
Verse	Characteristics of *"earthly, sensual, demonic"* Wisdom	Characteristics of *"wisdom that is from above"*
{13}		Good conduct, the meekness of wisdom (Meekness is not weakness, but it is wisely exercised strength.)
{14}	Bitter envy, self-seeking, boastful, lying	
{15}	Does not come from God	
{16}	Confusion and evil	
{17}		Pure, peaceable, gentle, willing to yield, full of mercy and good fruits… No partiality - No hypocrisy (We can relate these final two qualities to the argument in Antioch, which James solved in Acts, Chapter 13.)

Three Critical Principles

The Apostle Paul's writings teach us as much about walking in the fullness of the Holy Spirit as any other portion of the Bible. In the final section of this chapter, we will look at three critical principles from Romans, Chapter 8. They will help you to understand specific steps you can take to walk in continued access to divinely sourced wisdom.

1. LIVE ACCORDING TO HOW THE HOLY SPIRIT WANTS YOU TO LIVE.

   Romans 8:5-6 (NKJV)

   "For those who live according to the flesh set their minds on the things of the flesh, but those who live according to the Spirit, the things of the Spirit. {6} For to be carnally minded is death, but to be spiritually minded is life and peace."

This means that, in your daily life, you are to do your best to think spiritually, regardless of the carnal temptation to do otherwise. If you want continued access to the fullness of God's wisdom, measure your thinking against how the Holy Spirit asks you to think. Always trust His instructions. Give them priority over all carnal thoughts. Sometimes, the common sense you are used to relying upon has to defer (or give way) to God's kind of thinking. If you value this first principle, it will take you toward a constant, fullness of wisdom and understanding.

Guard the habit of thinking in a disciplined, wise and discerning way and act accordingly. Resist the temptation to second-guess yourself. Just trust God. As you do, refuse to base your faith on the outcomes you desire. Base it on knowing in whom it is that you trust.

Thinking as the Holy Spirit directs may not take you where you prefer to go, but it will keep you safely on track to fulfill the will of God. It will lead you to *"life and peace."*

2. BE LED IN ALL THINGS BY THE HOLY SPIRIT.

Romans 8:14 (NKJV)

"For as many as are led by the Spirit of God, these are sons of God."

You will have assurances that cannot be shaken, because they come from your heavenly Father.
- You will be assured that the Holy Spirit, Himself, has born witness and confirmed that you are a child of God.
- You will be assured that when you need to, you can cry *"Abba."* He will listen and respond, giving you His wisdom.
- You will be assured of God's wisdom, when you allow Him to lead you in every circumstance.

3. LIVE WITHOUT FEAR.

Romans 8:15-17 (NKJV)

"For you did not receive the spirit of bondage again to fear, but you received the Spirit of adoption by whom we cry out, "Abba, Father.""

{16} The Spirit Himself bears witness with our spirit that we are children of God, {17} and if children, then heirs; heirs of God and joint heirs with Christ, if indeed we suffer with Him, that we may also be glorified together."

You can live without fear because you have a privileged, family relationship with your heavenly Father. He is completely trustworthy and able to keep you safe and secure. His wisdom will never fail you. If you sense fear, look to God's leading. Fear is an emotion that tries to challenge, disrupt and overcome wise, godly thinking. When you are led by the Spirit of God, you have access to unrestrained, unlimited, endless wisdom. This includes knowing there is nothing to fear. It also includes knowing how to overcome specific situations that would tempt you to fear. This may sound lofty, but remember that you have access. It is a matter of total dependence and trust.

All of this means you can walk in the favor, grace, peace and continued access to the wisdom of God. Expect this and make it your constant prayer. When you receive it, use it for the good of those around you and of course, for God's glory.

You will enjoy all the benefits of your inheritance as a *"joint heir"* with Jesus, today and forever. Fear and even death will lose their dark uncertainties and painful stings. You will belong to God forever. As such, you can walk constantly, even eternally, in the fullness of what this means for you. God's kind of wisdom makes complete sense for a Christian.

Questions for Discussion

1. What might be the greatest value of personal diligence to guard your access to the wisdom God makes available to you?

2. What makes being *"willing to yield"* (James 3:17) qualify as *"wisdom from above?"* When you answer this, define *"willing to yield"* as part of your answer.

SEVEN

Uncommon Sense

We usually try to rely on common sense. Most of the time, this is the right thing to do. However, there will be times in every believer's life when it may not be the right thing to do. This happens when God asks us to step out in faith and obedience and do what may seem to be senseless or foolish. At these times, what you are asked to do will fly in the face of common sense. Instead, you will have to rely on what I call "uncommon sense." I will do my best to explain this to you. Let me begin with my personal testimony.

The year was 1997. I was the pastor of the Christian Mission Fellowship International Church in Suva, Fiji. It was a Thursday night and we met for our weekly elders' meeting at our home on Bureta Street in Suva. We ate together and then prayed. Then, we began to talk with each other about the business of the church. There were some things we desired to do, but we knew we did not have enough money in our church bank account to pay for them. It seemed that we had enough each week to meet our expenses, but never the extra money to expand into these additional outreach programs. We talked about how to raise some extra money. None of us in the elders' meeting could think of how we might get the financial resources we needed.

71

So, one of us suggested we do not try to come up with an answer that evening, but that we pray about it during the coming week. Then, when we got together for our next elders' meeting, we would discuss it again.

The following Thursday evening, we again met at our home. My wife, Nancy, prepared dessert for all of us, as was her custom for those evenings we met together as elders. We then had fellowship and prayed. Finally, it was time to get down to church business. I had not personally heard from the Lord in my prayers during the week, concerning how we might raise the money for the additional outreach programs we discussed in our last meeting. I asked the elders if any of them had heard from God about this. Nobody had, and so we still did not have an answer. There seemed to be no way for us to raise the additional funds we needed. At that moment, I did not understand why we had no ideas. So, we decided to spend even more time together praying in the meeting about it.

After some additional time in prayer, one of the elders, Bentley Wan said, *"I have it!"* well, that certainly captured our attention. The Holy Spirit put an incredible piece of "uncommon sense" into Bentley's heart, which he then shared with us. As he did, it was like a lightning bolt of grace and revelation that struck each of us. We were energized with faith and zeal. What God spoke through Bentley became a foundation for the principles by which I have lived through these many years that followed that meeting. It remains a foundational principle for my life today. Here is what

Bentley said: *"Let the church support an additional missionary!"*

Now, to our natural minds, spending more money defied common sense. This seemed to the natural ear to be nonsense, because we did not have the money in the church bank account. Fortunately, we were not listening with our natural ears. We had our spiritual ears tuned in to the Holy Spirit. Therefore, what we heard made "uncommon sense." After all, it came from our heavenly Father, who owns the cattle on a thousand hills. With one word, He could create streets paved with gold! He could fill the church bank account with whatever we needed... and so He did. If you have been around me for very long, you know one of my favorite sayings about the three names of God. *"His first name is "Faithful." His middle name is "Faithful." His last name is "Faithful." He is "Faithful, Faithful, Faithful!""* [7] That should make you shout!

Looking back on that moment, it is clear that it sometimes takes "uncommon sense" to hear God, obey without hesitation or question, and move ahead. It takes believing He is who He says He is and will do what He says He will do. What the Holy Spirit really spoke through Bentley that night was that we should look beyond what made common sense and open the eyes of our faith. Then, God would honor our obedience to support another missionary by answering our prayer. We ended up supporting two new missionaries. I know that these missionaries we began to support had been

---

[7] This saying originated from one of my elders in Fiji, Dr. Jide Olutamayin.

praying for provision and saw their prayers answered. I do not know for sure, but my guess is that they shouted too, just before they fell to their knees and thanked God. By the way, the Sunday after we made this decision, our offerings supernaturally increased and continued to grow from that point forward.

What is there to which you need to apply a little "uncommon sense"? It may take some determination and conviction. It may take the willingness to change some things. Go ahead. Just do it. Then start shouting... and do not bother to wait until you get your prayer answered. Shout by faith!

1 Corinthians 2:12-16 (NKJV)

"Now we have received, not the spirit of the world, but the Spirit who is from God, that we might know the things that have been freely given to us by God. {13} These things we also speak, not in words which man's wisdom teaches but which the Holy Spirit teaches, comparing spiritual things with spiritual. {14} But the natural man does not receive the things of the Spirit of God, for they are foolishness to him; nor can he know them, because they are spiritually discerned. {15} But he who is spiritual judges all things, yet he himself is rightly judged by no one. {16} For "who has known the mind of the Lord that he may instruct Him?" But we have the mind of Christ."

"Uncommon Sense" may be defined as, *"But we have the mind of Christ."*

1 Corinthians 2:16 is perfectly complimented by Romans 8:5. They both work together to reveal the potential we have to possess and exercise "uncommon sense."

1 Corinthians 2:16 (NKJV)

"For "who has known the mind of the Lord that he may instruct Him?" But we have the mind of Christ."

Romans 8:5b (NIV)

"...but those who live in accordance with the Spirit have their minds set on what the Spirit desires."

God always has the answers. We will have access to them as we determine to walk into an increasingly uncommon, deeper, relationship with Him. It will require faith in the face of what often appears to be foolish. However, God takes the foolish things and turns them into "uncommon sense," with extraordinary results. That is what walking in the fullness of the Holy Spirit is all about.

Questions for Discussion

1. What is the difference between common sense and "uncommon sense"?

2. In the testimony of the elders meeting, why was our decision to support another missionary so effective?

EIGHT

Uncommon Love

(Unrestrained, Unlimited and Endless *"agape"*)[8]

1 John 4:7-11 (NKJV)

"Beloved, let us love one another, for love is of God; and everyone who loves is born of God and knows God. {8} He who does not love does not know God, for God is love. {9} In this the love of God was manifested toward us, that God has sent His only begotten Son into the world, that we might live through Him. {10} In this is love, not that we loved God, but that He loved us and sent His Son to be the propitiation[9] for our sins. {11} Beloved, if God so loved us, we also ought to love one another."

John tells us *"In this is love,"* or as the original Greek language says, *"agape."*[10] *"Agape"* is an amazing word. It specifically refers to God's kind of love, according to the way He sees things, and according to what is in His heart. Nothing is common about the way God sees things. Nothing

---

[8] Portions of this chapter are taken from Dr. Abramson's book, "God's Kind of Love" © 2012, Robert Abramson.

[9] Propitiation means, to make it right for someone else - specifically, to pay the price for someone else's sin.

[10] Strong's Number G26.

is common about what is in His heart. John instructs us to infuse our relationships with love (*"agape"*) that is sourced from God. It is an extraordinary and completely "uncommon love." In God's kingdom, it is the norm. It is the stuff by which the fullness of the Holy Spirit manifests among us. In the dynamics of our world today, *"agape"* is entirely uncommon. Without it, we have wars, abuse and greed. We fall prey to countless other carnal tendencies and sinful behaviors.

God built us to thrive on love. It is what makes up the foundation of our humanity. Some of us simply do not know how to love, or to be loved. Some of us are just not equipped for it. At times, we fail to understand what love really is. People easily use expressions like, *"I love pizza,"* *"I love to swim,"* or *"I am falling in love."* The problem with *"falling in love"* is that it feels good until you stop falling, because you hit something. Ouch! As you can see, *"I love..."* has become a common expression that does not describe love accurately. "Uncommon love" has nothing to do with pizza, swimming or falling in a fallen world. It is an elevating, soaring experience in the Holy Spirit. Only loving as God loves will accurately define and demonstrate the meaning of biblical *"agape."* This statement below brings us to this primary truth of the Bible, which reveals its ultimate purpose.

John 3:16 (NKJV)

"For God so loved the world that He gave His only begotten Son, that whoever believes in Him should not perish but have everlasting life."

God's own example of this was the ultimate sacrificial act of giving us His Son. There is no greater gift than Jesus. This singular act of giving was the pivotal point in the fate of mankind. It opened the door to salvation and forever defined what "uncommon love" means. We cannot duplicate what the Father has done, but we can give people His love. A characteristic of walking in the fullness of the Holy Spirit is walking in such "uncommon love" (*"agape"*) that you will give up your greatest gift to others who have need of it.

An Empty Promise

A world that has redefined love has tried to dictate or determine our way of life. This way of life carries with it an empty promise that cannot fulfill our God-given hunger to love and be loved, as God loves (with *"agape"*). This way of life is increasing... and dangerously contagious! It has become part of contemporary society's expected and accepted norms for living. The world's kind of love is a counterfeit of the real thing, and is easy to identify.

- It is always selfish and makes self-centered demands.
- It is never commits to the needs and desires of others.
- It is hard-hearted and full of carnality.
- It is an emotionally charged urge to possess, or a desire to have an experience.
- It provides only temporary satisfaction.

Have you ever played Monopoly? It is a game that has similarities to the way many people go through life. Monopoly is played by advancing around a board and accumulating properties. The object is to gain an advantage over your friends by acquiring properties of the greatest strategic value. When you have done so, you wait for your friends to roll the dice and land on your properties. Each time they do, they pay you for their misfortune. As the game progresses, you do your best to take their properties and all their money. Eventually, and gleefully, you drive them off the board. They lose. You win! When the game is over, you put the game back in the box and close the lid.

When you have lived according to the world's kind of "Monopoly" love, and your time is finally over, they will put you in a box. Unfortunately, your time is *not* really over and you will find it very dark when they close the lid. However, if you lived life according to God's kind of love, "uncommon love," you will find a timeless, divinely sourced light waiting for you.

1 John 1:5-7 (NKJV)

"This is the message which we have heard from Him and declare to you, that God is light and in Him is no darkness at all. {6} If we say that we have fellowship with Him, and walk in darkness, we lie and do not practice the truth. {7} But if we walk in the light as He is in the light, we have fellowship with one another, and the blood of Jesus Christ His Son cleanses us from all sin."

Your life is to be a display of "uncommon love." Love in the same way God loves. You will find unlimited power to change lives for the better. Loving as God loves will bring you closer to the fullness of His Spirit in your life.

An Uncommon Promise with Uncommon Results

A life filled with "uncommon love" represents the heart of Christ and the fullness of His Spirit in you.

- It is based on the biblical truths you know, not on what you feel.
- It carries the compassion of Christ.
- It provides a path to a sense of fulfillment and purpose.
- It reflects the degree of access you have to the Holy Spirit.
- It represents how much you desire to be like Christ and show Him to the world.
- It is a walk with the Holy Spirit that will influence others to love as you do.

"Uncommon love," brings fellowship and forgiveness. It invites the Holy Spirit to open to you complete, continual access to His gifts, His way of thinking and especially, His heart. Love is not love unless it is a reflection of God! It is the purest, most amazing reflection and representation of Him. 1 John 4:8 (NKJV) says, *"God is love."*

Why is love so important? Why is *"agape"* so necessary to walking in the fullness of the Spirit? Why does constant access to it provide us with uncommon results? A close examination of the first three verses of 1 Corinthians 13 will give us the answers to these questions.

1 Corinthians 13:1-3 (NKJV)

"Though I speak with the tongues of men and of angels, but have not love, I have become sounding

81

brass or a clanging cymbal. {2} And though I have the gift of prophecy, and understand all mysteries and all knowledge, and though I have all faith, so that I could remove mountains, but have not love, I am nothing. {3} And though I bestow all my goods to feed the poor, and though I give my body to be burned, but have not love, it profits me nothing."

Verse 1 tells us that regardless of how or why we try to say the right thing, without God's kind of love in our hearts ("uncommon love") our words are nothing but loud, empty noises. Verse 2 tells us that even if we are highly gifted, really smart, and have incredible faith, without God's kind of love we are without substance. We are nothing but a big zero - absolutely nothing! Our hearts will not have access to the heart of God. Therefore, we cannot look forward to walking in the fullness of God's Spirit. Finally, Verse 3 reveals that even if we are extraordinarily charitable and helpful, and even if we sacrifice everything for the Lord, if we do it without love, we have gained nothing, and eventually will lose everything. These three verses of Scripture depict the emptiness of living without God's kind of love.

You cannot walk in the fullness of the Holy Spirit while denying the foundations of your life in Christ, which all rest on *"agape."* You cannot serve two masters, which are the world's love or God's kind of love. Another way to say this is that your love will be common to the world or it will be uncommon. This will be your choice. Will you embrace God's kind of "uncommon love"? If you will, the Holy

Spirit will open the gates to His fullness and offer you complete access. He will not leave you confused or without instruction concerning this offer. Here are the Holy Spirit's instructions (or you might say, His brief, concise directive) concerning the uncommon promise of His kind of love.

1 John 2:15-17 (NKJV)

"Do not love the world or the things in the world. If anyone loves the world, the love of the Father is not in him. {16} For all that is in the world; the lust of the flesh, the lust of the eyes, and the pride of life; is not of the Father but is of the world. {17} And the world is passing away, and the lust of it; but he who does the will of God abides forever."

Love is a Commandment leading to Constant Access to God.

Matthew 22:34-40 (NKJV)

"But when the Pharisees heard that He had silenced the Sadducees, they gathered together. {35} Then one of them, a lawyer, asked Him a question, testing Him, and saying, {36} "'Teacher, which is the great commandment in the law?" {37} Jesus said to him, "'You shall love the LORD your God with all your heart, with all your soul, and with all your mind.' {38} This is the first and great commandment. {39} And the second is like it: 'You shall love your neighbor as

yourself.' {40} "On these two commandments hang all the Law and the Prophets.""

A commandment is a requirement from God *"from which there is no retreat and about which there is no option."*[11] God looks at "uncommon love" as a spiritual requirement. In His eyes, it is not optional. To make "uncommon love" optional is to be in rebellion to God.

The power of "uncommon love" at work in you will demonstrate your determination to be just like Jesus. "Uncommon love" is released as you surrender to the leading of the Holy Spirit; and, reject the worldly ways around you. There are two clear and important advantages to having constant access to God's kind of love. These are illustrated in the Bible's Genesis narrative.

Genesis 2:15-18 (NKJV)

"Then the LORD God took the man and put him in the garden of Eden to tend and keep it. {16} And the LORD God commanded the man, saying, "Of every tree of the garden you may freely eat; {17} but of the tree of the knowledge of good and evil you shall not eat, for in the day that you eat of it you shall surely die." {18} And the LORD God said, "It is not good that man should be alone; I will make him a helper comparable to him.""

---

[11] Dr. Tom Peters, Senior Pastor of Trinity Church International, Lake Worth, Florida.

These two advantages are found in these verses. The first biblical illustration of the value of constant access to God's kind of love, and thus, the fullness of the Holy Spirit, is found in Verse 17. God gave Adam boundaries of safety. He also included a warning of how ignoring these boundaries would bring irreparable harm. The second is found in Verse 18. God provided for Adam's need for companionship. Unfortunately for Adam and Eve, and ultimately for all of us, they did not understand the value of their constant access to *"agape."* They rebelled and offended God. The result was that sin came into the world. Adam and Eve no longer had the blessing of their God-given boundaries of safety. Their relationship with each other, and with God, was no longer a constant reflection of pure *"agape"* love. Now their relationship began to reflect the damaged, sin-filled world in which they would have to live; and, through which they would have to navigate their lives.

Thousands of years later, with the coming of the New Covenant through Christ's blood sacrifice, we were restored to the possibility of the constant access Adam and Eve gave up. Following His resurrection and ascension, Jesus sent the Holy Spirit. This was a powerful demonstration of God's kind of love, resulting in a shower of divine grace. He provided us with the potential for living in the fullness of our relationship with God once again, just as it was before Adam and Eve sinned. On the following page, you will find my definition of God's kind of love.

> *God's kind of love, which is "uncommon love," is your intentional, consistent effort to bring as much of God's grace, His presence and His provision to someone, regardless of what it costs you.*

God's kind of love is always the agent through which there is a transfer of God's grace. Below, is my definition of grace. As you read it, you will see how it completely entwines with God's uncommon kind of love. They are two sides of the same coin.[12]

> *Grace is the divine expression of God's kind of love ("uncommon love"). Grace is what you could never do for yourself and only the Holy Spirit can do for you, and through you. It is sufficient for every circumstance. It is most often expressed through one person to another.*

"Uncommon love" will always provide open doors to the potential for you to shower someone with grace. Only when these doors are opened, will God's grace come in its fullness. Become His vessel of "uncommon love" and grace. You will take a giant step into the fullness of God's Spirit.

One of the most life-changing encounters I ever had, forever changed my understanding of "uncommon love." It was a request for prayer I received from a young Bible school student at Agape Renewal Center in Malaysia. He asked this

---

[12] As you read my other books or teachings on "agape," you will often find the same definitions of love and grace. I believe so strongly in them that they seem to find their way into the foundations of much of my writing.

of me: *"Would you pray that I could have the same love for people in my heart that you have shown us in your heart."*

God destined you to be captivated and transformed by "uncommon love." Then, you will be compelled to transfer that love and the grace it holds, from within yourself to someone else. The opportunity to dispense the grace of God makes us part of something far bigger than we are as individuals. It brings to mind Joseph's *"coat of many colours."*

Genesis 37:3 (KJV)

"Now Israel loved Joseph more than all his children, because he was the son of his old age: and he made him a coat of many colours."

Genesis 37:3b (NIV)

"...and he made a richly ornamented robe for him."

This description of a robe woven together in *"many colours"* that is *"richly ornamented,"* gives us a picture of the Body of Christ. We are all important threads in the divinely skillful weaving together of God's people. If one thread is snagged or pulled out, it destroys the integrity of the entire garment. What keeps all the threads in harmony and completes the image is "uncommon love."

Questions for Discussion

1. What would you add to the definitions of God's kind of love and grace that you just read?

2. What would you contribute to my thoughts on how "uncommon love" gives us constant access to the Holy Spirit? Explain how this can enhance our ability for each of us to walk in the fullness of the Holy Spirit.

NINE

Uncommon Commitment

(An Unrestrained and Unlimited Choice)

Commitment is always a choice. When I think about commitment, I cannot help but think about the contrasts the Bible presents to us. A very prominent and clearly contrasting Old Testament example is found in the Book of Ruth. Naomi and her two daughters-in-law, Orpah and Ruth, had all suffered the tragedy of losing their husbands. Now, they were widows. When Naomi decided to return to her people, one daughter-in-law, Orpah, turned away from her and chose to go back to her old life. However, Ruth would not abandon Naomi. She refused to walk away from her commitment to her mother-in-law, despite the difficulties they would face in their journey ahead. The Bible says that Ruth clung to Naomi. It was an "uncommon commitment." Ruth gave it without regard to what was ahead for them. Here is the moment of decision for both daughters-in-law, recorded in Scripture.

Ruth 1:14-16 (NKJV)

"Then they lifted up their voices and wept again; and Orpah kissed her mother-in-law, but Ruth clung to her. {15} And she said, "Look, your sister-in-law has gone back to her people and to

*her gods; return after your sister-in-law." {16}
But Ruth said: "Entreat me not to leave you, Or to
turn back from following after you; For wherever
you go, I will go; And wherever you lodge, I will
lodge; Your people shall be my people, And your
God, my God."*

Ruth illustrated that "uncommon commitment" never turns
back. It clings to whom it loves and walks faithfully into the
future. The great New Testament contrast to this may be
found in the Peter's denial of Christ at the Lord's time of
arrest and passion.

(Luke 22:54-62 NKJV)

*"Having arrested Him, they led Him and brought
Him into the high priest's house. But Peter
followed at a distance. {55} Now when they had
kindled a fire in the midst of the courtyard and sat
down together, Peter sat among them. {56} And a
certain servant girl, seeing him as he sat by the
fire, looked intently at him and said, "This man
was also with Him." {57} But he denied Him,
saying, "Woman, I do not know Him." {58} And
after a little while another saw him and said,
"You also are of them." But Peter said, "Man, I
am not!" {59} Then after about an hour had
passed, another confidently affirmed, saying,
"Surely this fellow also was with Him, for he is a
Galilean." {60} But Peter said, "Man, I do not
know what you are saying!" Immediately, while
he was still speaking, the rooster crowed. {61}*

And the Lord turned and looked at Peter. And Peter remembered the word of the Lord, how He had said to him, "Before the rooster crows, you will deny Me three times." {62} So Peter went out and wept bitterly."

Paraphrased, Peter said:

"I am choosing to refuse to honor my commitment to Jesus. I deny even knowing Him."

Peter did not cling to the Lord. He did not demonstrate "uncommon commitment." He distanced himself. When you distance yourself from whom or what you have committed to, you will be left with strong feelings of unpleasantness, and perhaps even shame, bitterness and sorrow.

Unlike Peter, Jesus gave us a model of "uncommon commitment." In the Garden of Gethsemane, just prior His passion, He demonstrated an unrestrained, unlimited and endless commitment to His heavenly Father. It could not be shattered by the knowledge He had of what was to come.

Luke 22:42 (NKJV)

"Father, if it is Your will, take this cup away from Me; nevertheless not My will, but Yours, be done."

Paraphrased, Jesus said:

"Father, I will stay committed to you through every painful moment that it will cost me. I will honor my commitment and honor You. I will not

flee. Instead, I will pin my pledge and obligation to you to the cross of my commitment, knowing it will live again with Me."

"Uncommon commitments" are unrestrained, unlimited and endless. Where do you find the strength to keep your commitments in all circumstances and under every kind of pressure? Here are some steps you can take to assure that you will find this strength:

1. Keep in step with your commitment. This means that you will need to walk it out and do whatever is required to stay fixed on it. Ruth did this. She chose to go on a long, dangerous journey with Naomi. God saw her heart and provided her the protection her commitment required.

2. Choose faith as your walking companion. Ruth had no idea what she would face. Her future was filled with uncertainty. Nevertheless, she put Naomi above what would have been her natural fears of the unknown. She said to Naomi, *"Your people shall be my people, And your God, my God."*[13] The Lord heard her promise and was pleased to be her God. He provided all she needed to honor her commitment and see that she walked into a future of certainty and blessings.

3. Like Jesus, just say "yes" to your commitment and refuse to say anything else. Open the door for the will of God to be done in your life.

---

[13] Ruth 1:16 (NKJV)

4. Do whatever it takes to honor your commitment. Do not compromise. Make and keep the commitment for whatever duration is necessary. When you know the season of your commitment has ended and your obligation has been fulfilled, you can move on. Jesus completed His task and emerged from the tomb three days later. He was victorious because He never compromised or denied His commitment.

5. Expect God to invade your commitment with His fully faithful response. God responded to both Ruth and Jesus in exactly the same way. He honored their commitments with His. In both situations, though very different, God the Father faithfully performed His Word. He is ready to perform His Word over your commitment, just as He always has for others.

"Uncommon commitment" produces winners and champions for Jesus. "Uncommon commitment" is determined to survive every trial and test, no matter how difficult or painful. Be a person of unrestrained and unlimited commitment. Your success and significance will validate your choice. It will open the gates to a walk in the fullness of the Holy Spirit. Along the way, you will *"walk worthy of the Lord, fully pleasing Him, being fruitful in every good work and increasing in the knowledge of God."*[14] Now, who could ask for a greater blessing or more opportunity to be a blessing?

---

[14] Colossians 1:10 (NKJV).

Questions for Discussion

1. What can you do to increase the strength of your commitments to God and others?
2. Are there pressures in the culture in which you live that may try to hinder you from keeping your commitments?

1 Walking according to the Spirit leads us out of slavery to sin and into liberty in Christ.

2 When we walk in the Spirit, our lives bear fruit that is fully pleasing to the Lord.

3 Living in the "fullness" of Holy Spirit takes us to our destinies, as we go from glory to glory.

4 "Fullness" means, "room for no more." (You have it all within you. Now, what you have will spill over onto others.)

5 Your future will be decided by the patterns and habits of your life.

6 Living at a normal level is for anyone. God has destined your life to be lived at the highest level.

7 Refuse to be denied, or accept the impossible as inevitable. The fullness of the Holy Spirit in your life will make all things possible.

8 God wants to speak to you even more than you want to hear Him. Listen carefully.

9 Worship is a demonstration that breaks chains and opens prison doors.

10 When you have an intimate relationship with God, the words you speak will have the potential to be unlimited in power.

11   When you have an intimate relationship with God, you will see far beyond the circumstances of the moment. You will not be alone. You will see Jesus.

12   The fullness of your faith and power will take others out of their personal prisons. (It might even deliver you from yours.)

13   When you demonstrate your faithfulness to God, You will see God's faithfulness respond to you... with power!

14   Miracles are demonstrations that challenge people to choose between Christ or doubt and unbelief.

15   If you want constant, unlimited power, surrender all that is necessary, so you can walk in the fullness of the Holy Spirit.

16   Do not waste an opportunity to ask God for what will enable you to make a difference for others. Then, when the Lord provides it, be sure to use it wisely.

17   Spiritual wisdom and understanding are effective tools. Sharpen them in your time with God.

18   Be wise and understanding about your rights and privileges as a child of God. Accept them, and the responsibilities that go with them.

19   Use the wisdom of God to make wise choices. As you do, you will have the correct and proper results.

20   Constant wisdom and understanding can be yours when you follow the Word of God.

21   God's kind of wisdom makes complete sense for a Christian.

22 "Uncommon sense" requires an uncommonly deep relationship with the Holy Spirit.

23 You have unlimited potential when you choose to be part of something bigger than yourself - the plan and purposes of God.

24 God destined you to be captivated and transformed by "uncommon love." Then, you will be compelled to transfer that love and the grace it holds, from within yourself to someone else.

25 "Uncommon commitment" never turns back. It clings to whom it loves; and, walks faithfully and faith-filled into the future.

26 When your commitments are unrestrained, unlimited and endless, they are so uncommon that, though they may seem lifeless, they will live again.

Part Two

The Nine Gifts of the Holy Spirit…For You

(From 1 Corinthians 12:4-11)

TEN

An Introduction to the Nine Gifts... For You

1 Corinthians 12:1 (NKJV)

"Now concerning spiritual gifts, brethren, I do not want you to be ignorant..."

1 Corinthians 12:4-11 (NKJV)

"There are diversities of gifts, but the same Spirit. {5} There are differences of ministries, but the same Lord. {6} And there are diversities of activities, but it is the same God who works all in all. {7} But the manifestation of the Spirit is given to each one for the profit of all: {8} for to one is given the word of wisdom through the Spirit, to another the word of knowledge through the same Spirit, {9} to another faith by the same Spirit, to another gifts of healings by the same Spirit, {10} to another the working of miracles, to another prophecy, to another discerning of spirits, to another different kinds of tongues, to another the interpretation of tongues. {11} But one and the same Spirit works all these things, distributing to each one individually as He wills."

God desires us to experience these nine gifts of the Holy Spirit. He wants us to understand their purpose and be effective in their use. 1 Corinthians 12:7 tells us that God provides these spiritual gifts individually to us, so we can use them for the good of our brothers and sisters in Christ. Verse 11 tells us that the Holy Spirit decides who gets a particular spiritual gift. (Of course, we may pray and ask for those gifts that have particularly touched our hearts.) Too many of us are not aware of what these nine spiritual gifts are, why they are given and how they can be used. Because of this, we choose not to ask for them or desire to use them.

As we begin to look at these nine gifts of the Holy Spirit, remember that nowhere in the Scriptures are they specifically defined, as they would be in a dictionary. They often overlap and operate together. Be careful not to put such tight labels on these gifts that you hinder your ability to be used by God. Keep an open mind. Be led by the Holy Spirit.

We will begin with brief summaries of the nine gifts. Then, we will look at them in depth in the following chapters. We can generally divide the nine gifts of the Spirit into three categories (though the categories may overlap and be used in concert with each other). Be aware that the order in which they occur in the Bible does not indicate one gift is more important than any other. They are all gifts from God that carry their own significance. All are unique and each has a valued place in the Kingdom of God.

The Three Revelation Gifts… For You

"Revelation" may be defined as, "God's disclosure of Himself and His will to His creatures."[15]

1. WORD OF WISDOM (1 Corinthians 12:8)

   A WORD OF WISDOM may be defined as a word, proclamation, or declaration that is supernaturally given through an individual by God. Its purpose is to meet the needs of a future occasion or problem. (These needs have not yet appeared, but will become apparent in the future.) Here are keys to look for that will help you recognize and properly define a WORD OF WISDOM.
   - Though God gives us natural wisdom, the Holy Spirit provides a WORD OF WISDOM in ways that are not revealed through human ability or natural wisdom. This wisdom is strictly sourced supernaturally through the Holy Spirit. It is God's revelation of His warnings, His direction concerning future opportunities, or His instructions concerning His plans and purposes.
   - It is given to one particular person through words, visions or dreams. He or she then speaks it. When spoken, it provides understanding and instruction on what action ought to be taken by another person or a group, concerning this future occasion.

2. WORD OF KNOWLEDGE (1 Corinthians 12:8)

   This spiritual gift communicates past or present facts or events that cannot be known through the natural senses of the speaker. A WORD OF KNOWLEDGE does not speak of

---

[15] Webster's College Dictionary - Word Genius.

the future. It is intended to acquire the listener's attention so that he or she is open to what the Holy Spirit is saying or doing next. A WORD OF KNOWLEDGE must be revealed to the speaker through the anointing of the Holy Spirit.

3. DISCERNING OF SPIRITS (1 Corinthians 12:10)

You may notice that this third revelation gift is not given in the list of nine spiritual gifts immediately following the first two. This has no bearing on its importance. DISCERNING OF SPIRITS is the supernatural recognition of the presence or activity of spiritual forces, either good or evil. DISCERNING OF SPIRITS is a particularly valuable gift in a world that tries to deny the presence of spiritual beings. DISCERNING OF SPIRITS may be considered a spiritual weapon. It will help you see what is happening in the supernatural that will affect your natural situation. (Be aware that DISCERNING OF SPIRITS is not a Christian's ability to sense or hear from the Holy Spirit. We all have been given that gift at the time we accepted Christ as our Lord and Savior.)

The Three Power Gifts… For You

"Power" refers to the supernatural power that comes from God. The power gifts of the Holy Spirit operate at levels that cannot be obtained by natural actions within the normal sphere of human experience. The hand of God exceptionally and completely sources them. They will require our cooperation and belief to function. Because they are filled with the fullness of the Holy Spirit, they may demonstrate His power without limitations. Some believers have formed doctrines that deny these gifts are in operation today.

Doctrines are man-made and may be flawed. The power gifts are given by God, who is never flawed and whose essence never changes.

4. FAITH (1 Corinthians 12:9)

As Christians, we are all given a measure of faith. FAITH, as listed in 1 Corinthians 12:9, is not normal faith. It is a supernaturally given, expressly elevated faith that God provides. You receive it for special occasions, needs and opportunities that require God's intervention in or through you. This special FAITH arises to do the following:

- It sustains those who receive it in times of persecution, hardship or imminent danger. Stephen had this gift as he preached to his soon-to-be murderers (Acts, Chapter 7). Paul and Silas received it in the Philippian jail (Acts, Chapter 16).
- It is also the faith God gives to some people who need to operate in extreme levels of power. Through these people, God does signs and wonders, and other unusual and amazing events. An example is Peter, as he and John walked past a crippled beggar, who had never walked (Acts, Chapter 3). Peter commanded the beggar to walk. Then he boldly took the man by the right hand, and pulled him up off the ground. As Peter did this, the man leaped up, walked into the temple, and praised God.

5. GIFTS OF HEALINGS (1 Corinthians 12:9)

These gifts (plural) are more than the believer's normal activity of praying for the sick or visiting a doctor. They are special gifts of healings, given to some Christians by which they have consistently positive results. They may, or may not be limited to a particular kind of disease or demonic oppression.

- These gifts are always supernatural. They often do the impossible. They accomplish miracle events.
- They may be done with prayer, but can include more than prayer, or can be a command or a touch.
- As the Apostle Paul did, certain people can recognize and use objects to bring God's healing. Two biblical examples are a shadow and a cloth.

6. WORKING OF MIRACLES (1 Corinthians 12:10)

The word *"miracles"* describes God's power, working independently or (as in 1 Corinthians 12:10) through a spiritual gift that His Spirit has given to a believer. The Greek word for *"miracles"* is *"dunamis."*[16] It may be defined as the working of God's power that interrupts, disregards and displaces the natural laws of nature. Therefore, the spiritual gift of WORKING OF MIRACLES refers to God using a person to disrupt His own design and order - to bring about His will. God's intention is that His supernatural intervention, through us, will apply WORKING OF MIRACLES (or any of the other gifts) to destroy the works of the devil.

The Three Vocal/Utterance Gifts... For You

7. PROPHECY (1 Corinthians 12:10)

Prophecy, as with all nine gifts of the Holy Spirit,

---

[16] Strong's Number G1411.

continues today. It includes two separate functions:

1. To foretell: This means to speak of things to come. These may be good tidings. They may be warnings of trouble. The trouble may or may not be judgment from God, but if the prophetic word is from Him, it will be accurate and true.

2. To forthtell: This means to bring correction and instruction as God's spokesperson, concerning a situation in the present time.

Both types of prophecy may come in the form of either the spoken or written word (or both at the same time). The Old Testament prophets, who were God's covenant enforcers, spoke more forthtelling than foretelling. Under the New Covenant, God still speaks to His church today through PROPHECY, both to foretell and forthtell. We do not view today's prophets with the same understanding as the Old Testament prophets. They are seen more as human messengers of the divine than as God's covenant enforcers.

8. DIFFERENT KINDS OF TONGUES (1 Corinthians 12:10)

This is the most prominent of the utterance gifts. It is a sign, given by the supernatural utterance of the Holy Spirit, through the tongue of a believer. DIFFERENT KINDS OF TONGUES are the initial evidence of being baptized in the Holy Spirit. This gift is used in public ministry and in our private times. It is primarily a devotional gift. DIFFERENT KINDS OF TONGUES may be spoken as a point of contact, communion and conversation between the believer and God.

9. INTERPRETATION OF TONGUES (1 Corinthians 12:10)

Tongues, when combined with interpretation, become the equivalent of prophecy. The interpretation comes by the inspiration of the Holy Spirit. INTERPRETATION OF TONGUES is given by God to us and through us, so we can edify believers, convict unbelievers of their sin, and show them that God is real.

The Holy Spirit uses these nine spiritual gifts from 1 Corinthians 12:4-11 to move supernaturally through the person He chooses. The gifts are intended to make our lives and those we touch with the nine gifts better. Below, we will look in depth at 1 Corinthians 12:11, as we unpack what Verse 11 teaches about how the Holy Spirit distributes His nine spiritual gifts.

Distribution of the Nine Gifts of the Holy Spirit

1 Corinthians 12:11 (NKJV)

"But one and the same Spirit works all these things, distributing to each one individually as He wills."

The Holy Spirit distributes the nine gifts to individual believers *"as He wills."* This means that He decides what gifts He gives and to whom He gives them. This does not stop us from asking Him for a particular gift. In fact, the Bible tells us to desire spiritual gifts (1 Corinthians 12:31). We all have a responsibility to ask for them. God has given us this opportunity. Asking for them is our right as believers. Remember, it is always Him operating through us. We must never take His glory by trying to take credit for a spiritual gift. Humility is our door to the power these gifts hold.

Every believer is called and empowered by the Holy Spirit to move in signs, wonders and the gifts of the Holy Spirit.

Understanding Your Spiritual Gifts
(They are *"special endowments."*)

1 Corinthians 12:1
(Literal Translation of the Greek New Testament)

"Now about spiritual gifts - the special endowments of supernatural energy, I do not want you to be uninformed or have any misunderstanding about them."

We cannot correctly operate in what we do not understand. If we understand the operation of the nine gifts of the Spirit, we should be able to explain their scriptural basis to others. Operating in the gifts of the Spirit is more than having feelings and enjoying the experiences. It is a demonstration of the power of God, through a willing vessel. Having the nine gifts of the Holy Spirit working in the church is God's plan for us until Jesus returns. We ought not to allow anyone or anything to tell us otherwise.

Hindrances to the Operation of the Nine Gifts of the Holy Spirit

1. THE TRADITIONS OF MEN

Religious traditions of many current denominations say the operation of the nine gifts of the Spirit ceased in the first century. These traditions would rob us of the miraculous, supernatural power of the Holy Spirit's gifts.

In Mark, Chapter 7, Jesus responded to the Pharisees, when they criticized His disciples for their lack of respect for tradition and doctrine. Jesus used the example of "corban." This was the practice of a person arranging to give his wealth and estate to the temple when he died, thus neglecting his aging parents. They were left with nothing. Jesus said the following about this evil tradition:

Mark 7:9, 13 (NKJV)

"...All too well you reject the commandment of God, that you may keep your tradition... {13} making the word of God of no effect through your tradition which you have handed down. And many such things you do."

Jesus said that the Pharisees made the Word of God of no effect through their traditions. They were breaking the Law of God in order to preserve the traditions of men. They denied what Paul would later write of as the ending of *"the law of sin and death"* and the advent of *"the law of the Spirit of life in Christ Jesus."* Under this New Covenant *"law"* we are free from those traditions that would require us to turn our backs on grace and remain in bondage. Refuse to let people or traditions rob you of the opportunity to operate in the gifts.

Romans 8:2 (NKJV)

"For the law of the Spirit of life in Christ Jesus has made me free from the law of sin and death."

Here are a number of additional hindrances to the operation of the nine gifts of the Holy Spirit.

2. LACK OF KNOWLEDGE (ignorance of God's Word)

Matthew 22:29 (NIV)

"Jesus replied, "You are in error because you do not know the Scriptures or the power of God."

3. NOT KNOWING THE GIVER OF THE GIFTS INTIMATELY

4. LACK OF DESIRE TO USE OUR SPIRITUAL GIFTS

We must not be spiritually lazy or lukewarm. We must be willing to nurture and express our spiritual gifts.

5. FEAR OF MAN

2 Corinthians 5:9 tells us our highest priority is to be *"well pleasing"* to God. If we fear that some person will not be pleased, we must not allow this fear to stop us from using our spiritual gifts. Jesus addressed this issue with His disciples. He said the following:

Matthew 10:28 (NKJV)

"And do not fear those who kill the body but cannot kill the soul. But rather fear Him who is able to destroy both soul and body in hell."

6. FEAR OF REJECTION

Subjecting ourselves to comparisons and being self-conscious will kill our ability to operate in the nine gifts of the Holy Spirit. We are all uniquely made to do exceptional things for God, without regard to what people might say or think.

7. FEAR OF MAKING A MISTAKE OR MISSING THE WILL OF GOD

A great responsibility comes with operating in the gifts of the Spirit. Take this responsibility very seriously. Then, allow God to move through you.

8. A LOW DEGREE OF FAITH

A low degree of personal faith will cause any of us to become susceptible to doubt and unbelief. It is a barrier to the boldness we need to operate in the nine gifts of the Holy Spirit.

Romans 12:6a (NKJV)

"Having then gifts differing according to the grace that is given to us, let us use them... in proportion to our faith;"

9. A LACK OF GENUINE, SELF-DENYING LOVE FOR OTHERS

Matthew 14:14 (NKJV)

"And when Jesus went out He saw a great multitude; and He was moved with compassion for them, and healed their sick."

The Scriptures repeatedly tell us that Jesus *"was moved with compassion."* If we are to be like Jesus, we must have the same kind of compassion toward others.

Are you being hindered from operating in the fullness of the gifts of the Holy Spirit? Decide today to identify anything that is preventing you from being a vessel of God.

1 Timothy 4:14 (NKJV)

"Do not neglect the gift that is in you, which was given to you by prophecy with the laying on of the hands of the eldership."

Ephesians 2:10 (NKJV)

"For we are all His workmanship, created in Christ Jesus for good works, which God prepared beforehand that we should walk in them."

Perspectives on the Nine Gifts of the Holy Spirit

We are to be open to God and sensitive to the Holy Spirit. As we obey the tasks God gives us to do, He accomplishes His will through us. If we are not obedient to the voice of God, we will probably not see a great measure of His nine gifts operating through us. You and I must submit to God. He wants to use us every day, in every way possible.

- Do not say, *"I cannot do it."* The truth is that you cannot do it yourself. God knows that. He wants to anoint you and work through you.
- Do not look back to the past or what you have not done.
- Do not look at your own abilities.
- Do not be self-centered. Your approach to the nine spiritual gifts must be God-centered.

When God gives you an assignment, the Holy Spirit will come and equip you for it. The key is not to focus on the gifts, but to recognize them as God moves through you. Focus on the Giver of the gifts! There is nothing more important than your relationship with God. Increase your

113

relationship with Him through loving communion and obedience. Then, you will find God using His gifts through you. His desire is two-fold:

1. He wants to be ever closer and more intimate with you.

2. He wants to use you more effectively for His purposes and His glory.

Your part is to do the following:
- Yield and obey!
- Receive and believe!
- Step out in faith and boldness!
- Exercise the gifts of God!

Questions for Discussion

1. How would you explain, in your own words, the three "Revelation Gifts?"

2. How would you explain, in your own words, the three "Power Gifts?"

3. How would you explain, in your own words, the three "Vocal/Utterance Gifts?"

4. Which of the nine hindrances listed in this chapter are generally the most limiting or challenging? Explain.

5. Is there any one of these nine hindrances that is the most personally challenging to you? If you desired to overcome this hindrance, which Scriptures would you turn to for guidance and assurance?

ELEVEN

The Three Revelation Gifts... For You

1 Corinthians 12:7-8, 10 (NKJV)

"But the manifestation of the Spirit is given to each one for the profit of all: {8} for to one is given the word of wisdom through the Spirit, to another the word of knowledge through the same Spirit..., {10} to another the working of miracles, to another prophecy, to another discerning of spirits, to another different kinds of tongues, to another the interpretation of tongues."

First Revelation Gift: WORD OF WISDOM

Here again is the definition given in the "Introduction to the Nine Gifts of the Holy Spirit." "A WORD OF WISDOM may be defined as a word, proclamation, or declaration that is supernaturally given through an individual by God. Its purpose is to meet the needs of a future occasion or problem. (These needs have not yet appeared, but will become apparent in the future.)"

Here again are keys to look for that will help you recognize and properly define a WORD OF WISDOM.

• "Though God gives us natural wisdom, the Holy Spirit

provides a WORD OF WISDOM in ways that are not revealed through human ability or natural wisdom. This wisdom is strictly sourced supernaturally through the Holy Spirit. It is God's revelation of His warnings, and His direction concerning future opportunities, or His plans and purposes.

- It is given to one particular person through words, visions or dreams. He or she then speaks it. When spoken, it provides understanding and instruction on what action ought to be taken by another person or a group, concerning this future occasion."

Why Do We Need a WORD OF WISDOM?

John 16:13 (NKJV)

"However, when He, the Spirit of truth, has come, He will guide you into all truth; for He will not speak on His own authority, but whatever He hears He will speak; and He will tell you things to come."

A WORD OF WISDOM, concerning the future, removes confusion, doubt or fear. It signals that God is aware and available. It gives clear understanding for decisions or actions. It can change a person's destiny. In Acts 27:22-26 Paul had a word of wisdom that reassured his shipmates that God would save them from the storm.

Acts 27:22-26 (NKJV)

"And now I urge you to take heart, for there will be no loss of life among you, but only of the ship.

116

{23} For there stood by me this night an angel of the God to whom I belong and whom I serve, {24} saying, 'Do not be afraid, Paul; you must be brought before Caesar; and indeed God has granted you all those who sail with you.' {25} Therefore take heart, men, for I believe God that it will be just as it was told me. {26} However, we must run aground on a certain island."

What follows is my personal testimony about an experience in which the Holy Spirit used me to deliver a WORD OF WISDOM. It was during a meeting, when I was the pastor of an international church in Fiji, that the Spirit of the Lord gave me this WORD OF WISDOM. During the service, I saw a vision of a hand in a piece of machinery. God spoke to me that there was a person in the congregation who would be in danger of injuring their hand at the workplace. I spoke this to the congregation.

There was a young woman present who worked in an office where they had a large printing press. Within the next few days, as she was working at the printing press, it malfunctioned. She began to put her hand into the machine to try to fix it. She suddenly remembered the WORD OF WISDOM I had spoken. She immediately pulled her hand back. It was just in time. The machine suddenly engaged itself. It came down where it would have mangled her hand, if she had not heeded the WORD OF WISDOM.

Second Revelation Gift: WORD OF KNOWLEDGE

1 Corinthians 2:12 (NKJV)

"Now we have received, not the spirit of the world, but the Spirit who is from God, that we might know the things that have been freely given to us by God."

As you read in the "Introduction to the Nine Gifts of the Holy Spirit," a WORD OF KNOWLEDGE "communicates past or present facts or events that cannot be known through the natural senses of the speaker. A WORD OF KNOWLEDGE does not speak of the future. It is intended to acquire the listener's attention, so that he or she is open to what the Spirit is saying or doing next."

There are two prevailing views in the church of what a WORD OF KNOWLEDGE is. The first view holds that a WORD OF KNOWLEDGE is what the Bible teaches us about God, Christ, the Gospel, and its applications to Christian living. This view is held in non-charismatic doctrines, by those who believe the nine gifts of the Holy Spirit are not for today. The second view, which is accepted by charismatic doctrines, and this author, holds that a WORD OF KNOWLEDGE comes directly from God. It acts like a laser beam, sent from the Holy Spirit, that strikes your heart with knowledge from heaven. The Holy Spirit does this through dreams, visions, or other supernatural means. It is the God-given, immediate awareness of facts without the aid of the natural senses. It is closely related to a WORD OF WISDOM. Many times, they are intertwined.

- It is God's revelation to you of any situation in the past or present that would be humanly impossible for you to know.
- It is knowledge that cannot be discovered by our five normal human senses, which are hearing, seeing, touching, smelling or tasting.

Ananias and Sapphira

Acts, Chapter 5 gives us the narrative in which Ananias lied to the church about his promise of a monetary gift. Peter considered that this was a lie, not to the church, but to the Holy Spirit. Peter did not know this by checking with public records or asking anyone. He knew Ananias lied, because he had a WORD OF KNOWLEDGE that the Holy Spirit had given him. Here is what Peter said. (Notice the reference to Satan filling Ananias' heart.)

Acts 5:3 (NKJV)

"But Peter said, "Ananias, why has Satan filled your heart to lie to the Holy Spirit and keep back part of the price of the land for yourself?""

Then, in Verse 9, Peter spoke a WORD OF WISDOM to Ananias's wife, Sapphira. He said, *"Look, the feet of those who have buried your husband are at the door, and they will carry you out."* God revealed to Peter that He was going to do the same thing to Sapphira that He did to Ananias. (Do you see how closely WORDS OF WISDOM and KNOWLEDGE can be to each other?)

Third Revelation Gift: DISCERNING OF SPIRITS

1 John 4:1-3 (NKJV)

"Beloved, do not believe every spirit, but test the spirits, whether they are of God; because many false prophets have gone out into the world. {2} By this you know the Spirit of God: Every spirit that confesses that Jesus Christ has come in the flesh is of God, {3} and every spirit that does not confess that Jesus Christ has come in the flesh is not of God. And this is the spirit of the Antichrist, which you have heard was coming, and is now already in the world."

As you read in the previous chapter, "DISCERNING OF SPIRITS is the supernatural recognition of the presence or activity of spiritual forces, either good or evil." It helps us uncover and identify things in the spirit realm.

1. It is not natural discernment. Everyone (saved or not) has a degree of natural discernment. Because an unbeliever cannot have a spiritual relationship with the Holy Spirit, he or she cannot have the spiritual gift of discernment from 1 Corinthians 12:10.

2. It is not spiritual mind reading. Only God can know what you are thinking. Trickery, manipulation, and the influence of ungodly familiar spirits, are often used to try to convince people that someone can read their minds. Nobody but God can read your mind!

3. It is not psychological insight. This kind of insight is valuable and can be learned from the proper education

and experience, but psychological insight is a completely natural skill.

4. It is not the power to discern fault in others in order to condemn them. Scripture forbids this. When we discern a problem in someone, it is to protect others or ourselves, or to help the person overcome their sinful behavior, so they can be restored to God.

Matthew 7:1 (NKJV)

"Judge not, that you be not judged."

Approach this issue of discernment with humility. It will keep you from trouble. It will give you the advantage that God wants you to have.

There are Five Kinds of Spirits.

1. The Spirit of God

2. Spirits from God (His angels)

3. Satan (the devil)

4. The spirits of the devil (his demons and antichrist spirits)

5. The spirit of man

DISCERNING OF SPIRITS, like the other spiritual gifts, is for a specific use at a specific occasion. DISCERNING OF SPIRITS goes beyond what you see in your natural circumstances. It allows you to see what is really beyond what your five natural senses are picking up. DISCERNING OF SPIRITS helps you form sound judgments based on spiritual insight.

- It is not based on what you can figure out for yourself.
- It is not knowledge that you have been taught.

DISCERNING OF SPIRITS gives you the ability to discern false teachers, false prophecies and false doctrine.

1 Timothy 4:1 (NKJV)

"Now the Spirit expressly says that in latter times some will depart from the faith, giving heed to deceiving spirits and doctrines of demons,"

When false doctrine is preached, taught and then believed, it puts a person's eternal life and the quality of his or her everyday life in danger. Ask the Lord to help you discern the spirits when you read books, use the internet, listen to the radio, watch TV or a movie. Discern the spirits when you listen to someone who you do not know, who is preaching or teaching in public meetings. Not everyone in a pulpit or podium is delivering true doctrine.

DISCERNING OF SPIRITS exposes demonic spirits. Once exposed, these spirits can be dealt with, and people can be set free. Acts, Chapter 16 gives us a classic, clear example of how the Apostle Paul discerned that it was not an unfortunate slave girl who was mocking him and his friends, but an unholy spirit that possessed her.

Acts 16:16-18 (NKJV)

"Now it happened, as we went to prayer, that a certain slave girl possessed with a spirit of divination met us, who brought her masters much profit by fortune-telling. {17} This girl followed

Paul and us, and cried out, saying, "These men are the servants of the Most High God, who proclaim to us the way of salvation." {18} And this she did for many days. But Paul, greatly annoyed, turned and said to the spirit, "I command you in the name of Jesus Christ to come out of her." And he came out that very hour."

DISCERNING OF SPIRITS also gives us the ability to discern the spiritual source of some sicknesses and diseases. The Gospels and the Book of Acts validate that there may be spiritual causes to sickness. Here is one example from Acts:

Acts 10:38 (NKJV)

"how God anointed Jesus of Nazareth with the Holy Spirit and with power, who went about doing good and healing all who were oppressed by the devil, for God was with Him."

DISCERNING OF SPIRITS often leads to deliverance or healing. However, the ability to discern spirits is not followed automatically by the casting out of demons. Every believer has the potential to minister deliverance, but you had better know what you are doing before trying.

1. You must be spiritually prepared.

2. The person being delivered must (1) repent, (2) want to be delivered, (3) want to close his or her heart to demonic activity; and, (4) actively pursue God.

3. The demon must recognize that you walk in God's authority. If your life does not reflect this, stay away from confronting demons.

4. You must be born again and spiritually prepared. Otherwise, you will put yourself in serious danger by trying to cast out demons. Once again, Acts gives us an example of this:

Acts 19:13-16 (NKJV)

"Then some of the itinerant Jewish exorcists took it upon themselves to call the name of the Lord Jesus over those who had evil spirits, saying, "We exorcise you by the Jesus whom Paul preaches." {14} Also there were seven sons of Sceva, a Jewish chief priest, who did so. {15} And the evil spirit answered and said, "Jesus I know, and Paul I know; but who are you?" {16} Then the man in whom the evil spirit was leaped on them, overpowered them, and prevailed against them, so that they fled out of that house naked and wounded."

Questions for Discussion

1. Are you clear concerning the difference between a WORD OF WISDOM and a WORD OF KNOWLEDGE? Explain it in your own terms.

2. Do you ever have difficulty believing that there is really a devil and demons? If so, what causes this? If not, what would you say to someone who does not believe?

TWELVE

The Three Power Gifts... For You

1 Corinthians 12:4, 9-10 (NKJV)

"There are diversities of gifts, but the same Spirit... {9} to another faith by the same Spirit, to another gifts of healings by the same Spirit, {10} to another the working of miracles, to another prophecy, to another discerning of spirits, to another different kinds of tongues, to another the interpretation of tongues."

First Power Gift: FAITH

The gift of FAITH is neither saving faith nor general faith. It is extraordinary mountain-moving faith. It is God-given special faith for supernatural results in a specific situation. This faith arises to do the following:

- It sustains those that receive it in times of persecution, hardship or imminent danger. Stephen had this gift as he preached to his soon-to-be murderers (Acts, Chapter 7).
- It is also the faith God gives to those who operate in extreme levels of power. Through these people, God consistently does signs and wonders, and other unusual and amazing events.

When we receive this gift of FAITH, it empties us of all doubt and unbelief. It is given by God to whom He wills, as a supernatural supply of faith that goes beyond "ordinary" faith. People with this extraordinary gift of FAITH expect great things from God. They do not look to a promise, but to the One who makes the promise. This is an elevated level of faith. It releases God's power beyond normal expectations. It is an unusual explosion of power. It displays complete assurance and trust in God, no matter what the circumstances may be. Daniel had this gift in the lion's den.

Daniel 6:23 (NKJV)

"Then the king was exceedingly glad for him, and commanded that they should take Daniel up out of the den. So Daniel was taken up out of the den, and no injury whatever was found on him, because he believed in his God."

Outrageous Faith

There are times when our faith needs to stretch to the point where it can be described as outrageous. I found an example of this in an article by Ernie Gross. It was published in "This Day in Religion" in 1990. I would like to share it with you:

"In 1540, Martin Luther's good friend and assistant, Friedrich Myconius, became sick and was expected to die within a short time. From his bed, he wrote a tender farewell letter to Luther. When Luther received the message, he immediately sent back a reply. He replied with the gift of faith. Here is Luther's reply. *"I command*

you in the name of God to live because I still have
need of you in the work of reforming the church.
The Lord will never let me hear that you are dead,
but will permit you to survive me. For this I am
praying, this is my will, and may my will be done,
because I seek only to glorify the name of God."
God gave Martin Luther this outrageous gift of
FAITH. Although Myconius had already lost the
ability to speak when Luther's reply came, he
recovered. He lived six more years. He died two
months after Luther died."[17]

While pastoring and teaching in the Fiji Islands, my students
told me a story about my Assistant Pastor, Emitai Ratalatala.
It occurred when he led a missionary team in Papua New
Guinea. Here is the story as it happened:

Emitai and his team were crossing mountains and
rivers to reach a people far into the interior of
Papua New Guinea. They came to a river full of
crocodiles. There was a small boat for hire to get
people and their goods safely across. The team
only had enough money for one trip across. A
single trip would not get both them and their
equipment across. The boat was too small. Emitai
gathered his team and said, *"We're going to pray*
and put the equipment on the ferry. Then, we will
swim." He told me they safely swam through the
crocodile infested waters and arrived at the other
side.

---

[17] Gross, Ernie. *This Day in Religion.* New York: Neal-Schuman, © 1990.

When the story ended, Emitai said, *"We swam with great faith... but we swam really fast!"* We all had a good laugh. (Even the gift of FAITH never takes God's grace for granted.) The gift of this special kind of faith expects and trusts in the supernatural intervention of God, even while it does its best to cooperate with His will.

Second Power Gift: GIFTS OF HEALINGS
(These gifts are described in plural terms.)

1 Corinthians 12:9 (NKJV)

"to another faith by the same Spirit, to another gifts of healings by the same Spirit,"

1 Corinthians 12:28, 30 (NKJV)

"And God has appointed these in the church: first apostles, second prophets, third teachers, after that miracles, then gifts of healings, helps, administrations, varieties of tongues... {30} "Do all have gifts of healings?""

These gifts (again, plural) are different from times when we normally pray for the sick, or visit a doctor. These are supernatural events with consistently supernatural outcomes. God gives GIFTS OF HEALINGS to some Christians who then have consistently miraculous results. They may include more than prayer. As it was with the Apostle Paul, these gifts can manifest in the use of objects that were endowed with healing (Acts 19:11-12). Even the presence of people with these gifts, without saying or doing anything, can bring healing. An example of this is Peter's shadow (Acts 5:15).

Sickness was not a part of God's original plan for us.

- There was no drug store in the Garden of Eden.
- There was no hospital in the Garden of Eden.
- There was no aspirin bottle in the Garden of Eden.

In the Garden of Eden, God called to Adam and said, *"Where are you?"* Adam did not reply, *"I'm in bed with a fever. My nose is dripping and I am having a problem with my arthritis."* There was no sickness in the garden. With the fall of Adam, however, sin brought sickness and death.

Psalm 103:2-4 (NKJV)

"Bless the LORD, O my soul, And forget not all His benefits: {3} Who forgives all your iniquities, Who heals all your diseases, {4} Who redeems your life from destruction, Who crowns you with lovingkindness and tender mercies,"

Healing is more than just the physical deliverance from sickness. God also heals emotional hurts and sickness.

Psalm 147:3 (NKJV)

"He heals the brokenhearted And binds up their wounds."

Jesus is the Healer

Matthew 4:23-24 (NKJV)

"And Jesus went about all Galilee, teaching in their synagogues, preaching the gospel of the kingdom, and healing all kinds of sickness and all

129

kinds of disease among the people. {24} Then His fame went throughout all Syria; and they brought to Him all sick people who were afflicted with various diseases and torments, and those who were demon-possessed, epileptics, and paralytics; and He healed them."

"The Spirit of the LORD is upon Me, Because He has anointed Me To preach the gospel to the poor; He has sent Me to heal the brokenhearted, To proclaim liberty to the captives And recovery of sight to the blind, To set at liberty those who are oppressed; {19} To proclaim the acceptable year of the LORD."

The root of the world's sickness is sin. Sickness may also be the result of demonic activity or naturally occurring diseases. These afflict us because we live in a corrupted, fallen, sin-filled world. All sicknesses and disease are bondage and oppression.

Luke 13:10-16 (NKJV)

"Now He was teaching in one of the synagogues on the Sabbath. {11} And behold, there was a woman who had a spirit of infirmity eighteen years, and was bent over and could in no way raise herself up. {12} But when Jesus saw her, He called her to Him and said to her, "Woman, you are loosed from your infirmity." {13} And He laid His hands on her, and immediately she was made straight, and glorified God. {14} But the ruler of

the synagogue answered with indignation, because Jesus had healed on the Sabbath; and he said to the crowd, "There are six days on which men ought to work; therefore come and be healed on them, and not on the Sabbath day." {15} The Lord then answered him and said, "Hypocrite! Does not each one of you on the Sabbath loose his ox or donkey from the stall, and lead it away to water it? {16} So ought not this woman, being a daughter of Abraham, whom Satan has bound; think of it; for eighteen years, be loosed from this bond on the Sabbath?""

Acts 10:38 (NKJV)

"how God anointed Jesus of Nazareth with the Holy Spirit and with power, who went about doing good and healing all who were oppressed by the devil, for God was with Him."

Physical healing, health and well-being were obtained for us on the cross of Christ. The work was complete and lacked nothing in its effectiveness.

Isaiah 53:5 (NKJV)

"But He was wounded for our transgressions, He was bruised for our iniquities; The chastisement for our peace was upon Him, And by His stripes we are healed."

Matthew 8:17 (NKJV)

"...that it might be fulfilled which was spoken by

131

Isaiah the prophet, saying: "He Himself took our infirmities And bore our sickness.""

1 Peter 2:24 (NKJV)

"who Himself bore our sins in His own body on the tree, that we, having died to sins, might live for righteousness; by whose stripes you were healed."

Below are suggestions for how you should function in the anointing with GIFTS OF HEALINGS.

1. PREPARE YOURSELF SPIRITUALLY.
   - Spend time in prayer, specifically aimed at healing.
   - Learn the healing Scriptures. Then, at any time, you can use the power of the Word of God to pray for someone's healing.
   - Stay in close relationship with the Holy Spirit. You will be prepared when He directs you to pray.

2. BE MOTIVATED BY LOVE AND COMPASSION.
   Jesus was moved with compassion when He healed people. Get compassion in your heart before you pray.

1 Corinthians 13:1-2 (NKJV)

"Though I speak with the tongues of men and of angels, but have not love, I have become sounding brass or a clanging cymbal. {2} And though I have the gift of prophecy, and understand all mysteries and all knowledge, and though I have all faith, so that I could remove mountains, but have not love, I am nothing"

3. APPLY THESE STEPS TO YOUR HEALING MINISTRY.
- Find out the reason someone needs healing.
- Ask if he or she believes it is God's will they be healthy.
- Ask if the person is a believer. (Salvation is more important than healing, and often the first step to it.)
- Ask if he or she believes that Jesus can heal them.
- Ask the Holy Spirit for a WORD OF KNOWLEDGE or WORD OF WISDOM about the situation before you pray.
- Inquire whether there is unforgiveness or bitterness toward someone?
- After praying, when the healing has manifested, direct the glory and praise to the Lord. If it has not yet manifested, do the same. Give God glory and praise.
- In those occasions when the healing has not immediately manifested, encourage the person to stand on the Word of God and resist the devil.

Third Power Gift: WORKING OF MIRACLES

I Corinthians 12:10a (NKJV)

"...to another the working of miracles,"

As you read earlier, "The word *"miracles"* describes God's power, working independently or (as in 1 Corinthians 12:10) through a spiritual gift that His Spirit has given to a believer. The Greek word for *"miracles"* is *"dunamis."*[18] It may be defined as the working of God's power that interrupts, disregards and displaces the natural laws of nature.

---

[18] Strong's Number G1411.

Therefore, the spiritual gift of WORKING OF MIRACLES refers to God using a person to disrupt His own design and order - to bring about His will. God's intention is that His supernatural intervention, through us, will apply WORKING OF MIRACLES (or any of the other gifts) to destroy the works of the devil."

Rev. Kenneth Hagin wrote, *"Working of miracles is not a passive gift. It acts to do the miracle."*[19] Though God performs the miracle, it almost always requires someone to believe and then take personal action. When God's power works through a person's gift, He interrupts the way things naturally occur. Through the person He uses, God disrupts His own design and order. All of God's miracles will exalt Jesus. Again, a biblical example of this is found in Acts, Chapter 19. It reported that people took handkerchiefs and aprons that had been in contact with the Apostle Paul, and brought them to the sick. These were compassionate, deliberate, personal actions.

Acts 19:11 (NKJV)

"Now God worked unusual miracles by the hands of Paul, [12] so that even handkerchiefs or aprons were brought from his body to the sick, and the diseases left them and the evil spirits went out of them."

The Scriptures also use the terms *"signs"* and *"wonders"* (often together) in reference to the divine acts of God.

---

[19] Hagin, Kenneth, The Holy Spirit and His Gifts, P.119.

Mark 16:20 (NKJV)

"And they went out and preached everywhere, the Lord working with them and confirming the word through the accompanying signs. Amen."

Acts 14:3 (NKJV)

"Therefore they stayed there a long time, speaking boldly in the Lord, who was bearing witness to the word of His grace, granting signs and wonders to be done by their hands."

Beware of Lying Wonders - Beware!

The Scriptures warn us that what may appear to be miracles, signs and wonders may be the work of evil deception. Be careful not to accept at face value, what appears to be a miracle unless you have asked the Holy Spirit to confirm what you have seen. Your heart will not lie to you, if you allow Him to speak to it.

Matthew 24:24 (NKJV)

"For false Christs and false prophets will appear and perform great signs and miracles to deceive even the elect--if that were possible."

2 Thessalonians 2:9 (NKJV)

"The coming of the lawless one...according to the working of Satan, with all power, signs, and lying wonders"

The Greatest Miracle

The greatest miracle was God coming to earth, born of a virgin. He was fully human, yet never lost His divine attributes. He voluntarily veiled them, but always remained fully God. About thirty years later, when the Holy Spirit came upon Jesus, He unveiled some of His divine attributes. When He arose from the dead, He unveiled all of them. Now, He is alive and active with all His miraculous power.

Our greatest miracle is our salvation experience. Do you know Jesus as your personal Lord and Savior?

Ephesians 2:8-9 (NKJV)

"For by grace you have been saved through faith, and that not of yourselves; it is the gift of God, {9} not of works, lest anyone should boast."

2 Corinthians 5:17(NKJV)

"Therefore, if anyone is in Christ, he is a new creation; old things have passed away; behold, all things have become new."

Questions for Discussion

1. What would your response be to people who ask you why they prayed, but healing was not manifested? Do you have an answer that you could support with Scripture?

2. In your opinion, why do many cultures not see the gift of WORKING OF MIRACLES very often, if at all?

THIRTEEN

The Three Vocal/Utterance Gifts... for You

First Vocal/Utterance Gift: PROPHECY

1 Corinthians 12:10b (NKJV)

"...to another prophecy, to another discerning of spirits, to another different kinds of tongues, to another the interpretation of tongues."

This Chapter of our study of the nine gifts of the Holy Spirit will focus on the New Testament gift of PROPHECY.[20] As you read earlier, the gift of PROPHECY continues today. Under the New Covenant, it has two separate functions. First, it foretells or speaks of things to come. These may be good tidings or may be warnings of trouble. A prophetic word from God will be accurate and true, and should be considered carefully. Second, a prophetic word may forthtell, or bring correction and instruction through God's spokesperson in the present time. Both these types of prophecy may come in the form of either a spoken or a written word.

PROPHECY may be defined as a message from God, imparted by the Holy Spirit, delivered through one of His servants,

---

[20] We will not examine the subject of Old Testament prophecy, nor the office of the Old Testament prophet.

either by speaking or writing. We view today's prophets, or people with a prophetic word, as messengers. We may receive a prophetic message from God at any time. PROPHECY is divinely given so we can ponder what God has said and determine whether we should share it. PROPHECY is different from preaching or teaching, although there are times when people preach or teach prophetically, or prophesy as part of a sermon or in the altar ministry. In these times, we are able to receive what God has delivered through their ministry.

PROPHECY is a gift given to Christians who may, or may not hold a five-fold ministry office. We will draw our information from 1 Corinthians 14:1-32 which is provided for your reference, below.

1 Corinthians 14:1-32 (NKJV)

"Pursue love, and desire spiritual gifts, but especially that you may prophesy. {2} For he who speaks in a tongue does not speak to men but to God, for no one understands him; however, in the spirit he speaks mysteries. {3} But he who prophesies speaks edification and exhortation and comfort to men. {4} He who speaks in a tongue edifies himself, but he who prophesies edifies the church. {5} I wish you all spoke with tongues, but even more that you prophesied; for he who prophesies is greater than he who speaks with tongues, unless indeed he interprets, that the church may receive edification. {6} But now, brethren, if I come to you speaking with tongues, what shall I profit you unless I speak to you either

by revelation, by knowledge, by prophesying, or by teaching? {7} Even things without life, whether flute or harp, when they make a sound, unless they make a distinction in the sounds, how will it be known what is piped or played? {8} For if the trumpet makes an uncertain sound, who will prepare himself for battle? {9} So likewise you, unless you utter by the tongue words easy to understand, how will it be known what is spoken? For you will be speaking into the air. {10} There are, it may be, so many kinds of languages in the world, and none of them is without significance. {11} Therefore, if I do not know the meaning of the language, I shall be a foreigner to him who speaks, and he who speaks will be a foreigner to me. {12} Even so you, since you are zealous for spiritual gifts, let it be for the edification of the church that you seek to excel. {13} Therefore let him who speaks in a tongue pray that he may interpret. {14} For if I pray in a tongue, my spirit prays, but my understanding is unfruitful. {15} What is the conclusion then? I will pray with the spirit, and I will also pray with the understanding. I will sing with the spirit, and I will also sing with the understanding. {16} Otherwise, if you bless with the spirit, how will he who occupies the place of the uninformed say "Amen" at your giving of thanks, since he does not understand what you say? {17} For you indeed give thanks well, but the other is not edified. {18} I thank my God I speak with tongues more than you all; {19} yet in the church I would rather speak five words with my understanding, that I may teach others also, than ten thousand words in a tongue. {20} Brethren, do not be children in understanding; however, in malice be babes, but in understanding be mature. {21} In the law it is written: "With men of other tongues and other lips I will speak to this people; And yet, for all that, they will not hear Me," says the Lord. {22} Therefore tongues are for a sign, not to those who believe but to unbelievers; but prophesying is not for unbelievers but for those who believe. {23} Therefore if the whole church comes together in one place, and all speak with tongues, and there come in those who are uninformed or unbelievers, will they not say that you are out of your mind? {24} But if all prophesy, and an unbeliever or an uninformed person comes in, he is convinced by all, he is convicted by all. {25} And thus the secrets of his heart are revealed; and so, falling down on his face, he will worship God and report that God is truly among you. {26} How is it then, brethren? Whenever you come together, each of you has a psalm, has a teaching, has a tongue, has a revelation, has an interpretation. Let all things be done for edification. {27} If anyone speaks in a tongue, let there be two or at the most three, each in turn, and let one interpret. {28} But if there is no interpreter, let him keep silent in church, and let him speak to himself and to God. {29} Let two or three prophets speak, and let the others judge.

{30} But if anything is revealed to another who sits by, let the first keep silent. {31} For you can all prophesy one by one, that all may learn and all may be encouraged. {32} And the spirits of the prophets are subject to the prophets."

Now, let's look carefully at some of these verses from 1 Corinthians 14.

1 Corinthians 14:1(NKJV)

"Pursue love, and desire spiritual gifts, but especially that you may prophesy."

We are encouraged to prophesy. God is pleased when we have such a desire and step out in faith, under the guidance of others in authority, to learn to use the gift. The Bible instructs us to seek the gift of PROPHECY, so that we can edify the body of Christ.

In 1993, I experienced my first challenge with the gift of PROPHECY. Here is the story:

I had been invited to go to New Zealand and teach in a Bible school that trained students from around the world to be missionaries and pastors. It was a wonderful experience, but part of the invitation was that I would participate in my first prophetic presbytery. It would take place prior to the Bible school graduation. I agreed on the condition that if I had nothing to say, I would not be pressured to get up and say even one word. The people who invited me agreed.

On the morning of the presbytery, I found myself sitting in the meeting, waiting alongside the men who were to work with me. I was nervous and unsure how the morning would develop. I had no great anticipation that I would operate in the gift of PROPHECY. The presbytery was set up so each student would come forward and sit in a chair. The three of us who were to prophesy would be sitting in the first row facing the student. When one of us had a prophetic word, he would look to the others and defer to them as necessary. If they nodded approval, he was to get up and begin to prophesy.

There I sat, with no feeling of anything unusual and no sense of anointing. The first student came forward and sat in the chair. To my great surprise, I heard the voice of the Lord in my heart. He clearly said, *"This man is a builder."* That is the only thing I heard. The other two men, who were seasoned in prophecy, just sat there as I considered what I had heard. Then, I found myself compelled to get up and walk over to the student. I checked with the other two men and they nodded at me. So, I got up and stood by the student's chair. I said the only thing I had heard, *"You are a builder. You will build God's kingdom and go many places in the world to do so."* Then, I walked back to my seat and sheepishly sat down.

One of the other men I was sitting with was familiar with this student. He leaned over and said to me, *"This man has been a home builder for many years and has come to Bible school to prepare to be a missionary builder. He wants to travel the world, building churches and ministry facilities.*" I was startled at this, but did not have much time to reflect on what had happened. I found myself engaged in the prophetic process and have never been the same. I realized God had given me the gift of PROPHECY. He had moved me one step closer to walking in the fullness of the Holy Spirit.

The Purposes of Prophecy

"edification, exhortation and comfort to men"

1 Corinthians 14:2-3(NKJV)

"For he who speaks in a tongue does not speak to men but to God, for no one understands him; however, in the spirit he speaks mysteries. {3} But he who prophesies speaks edification and exhortation and comfort to men."

Prophecy is not like tongues. Tongues do not speak to men. Tongues are only understood by God. The Bible calls what we say when speaking in tongues *"mysteries."* Prophecy speaks clearly to people. It is understandable and certain. Verse 3 gives us God's purposes for prophecy. There are three specific Scriptural goals He has for us, as we prophesy. They are: (1) edification, (2) exhortation and (3) comfort. Looking at each one of these will give us insight into the mind of God as He provides the gift of PROPHECY in today's church.

1. EDIFICATION

To edify means, *"to instruct, uplift or enlighten."*[21] God always intends to draw those who receive edification closer to Him. According to Verse 3, prophetic words bring this edification. We are never to prophesy to bring condemnation. Speaking condemnation through the gift of PROPHECY is not a normative New Testament principle. There may be a time when God requires a prophet to speak what may be perceived as harsh words, but it would be highly unusual. On these rare occasions, it must be done with fear and trembling, taking care never to be judgmental. Edification is God's desire for His children. He says this through the following verse:

1 Corinthians 14:4-5 (NKJV)

"Even so you, since you are zealous for spiritual gifts, let it be for the edification of the church that you seek to excel. {5} I wish you all spoke with tongues, but even more that you prophesied; for he who prophesies is greater than he who speaks with tongues, unless indeed he interprets, that the church may receive edification."

Prophecy edifies both individuals and the church body. There are two Greek words that give us the English words *"edify"* and *"edification."* They are *"oikodomeo"* and *"oikodome."*[22] They share the same Greek root (*"doma"*). Together they mean, *"to be a house-builder, to construct or strengthen, embolden and encourage."*

---

[21] Webster's College Dictionary - Word Genius.
[22] Strong's Number G3619. This is a compilation of G3624 and the base of G1430.

Skipping ahead to Verse 12, you have indisputable confirmation that God's first purpose for a person to have the gift of PROPHECY is to edify the church.

1 Corinthians 14:12 (NKJV)

"Even so you, since you are zealous for spiritual gifts, let it be for the edification of the church that you seek to excel."

2. EXHORTATION

To exhort is *"to urge, advise, caution earnestly; or to admonish urgently."*[23] This does not exclude the possibility that there may be temporary discomfort, until those who receive the word of exhortation respond by making whatever changes are necessary. Discomfort happens because God desires that our lives always agree with His plans, His Word and His love for us. Lifestyles that are independent from God may cause discomfort or worse. When accepted and acted upon, a word of exhortation can bring us into agreement with God. It can give us entrance into a deeper relationship with Him and access to the fullness of His Spirit.

3. COMFORT

To comfort is *"to soothe, console, or reassure; bring solace or cheer."*[24] The gift of PROPHECY is intended by God to bring comfort to those who receive it.

---

[23] Webster's College Dictionary - Word Genius.
[24] ibid.

4. WE CAN LEARN FROM IT.

1 Corinthians 14:6 (NKJV)

"But now, brethren, if I come to you speaking with tongues, what shall I profit you unless I speak to you either by revelation, by knowledge, by prophesying, or by teaching?"

Do not disregard or discard a word of prophecy at a time when its message can deliver a life-changing teachable moment to you. God knows precisely what you need to hear from Him at the exact time you need it.

5. PROPHECY BRINGS UNBELIEVERS TO REPENTANCE.

1 Corinthians 14:24-25 (NKJV)

"But if all prophesy, and an unbeliever or an uninformed person comes in, he is convinced by all, he is convicted by all. {25} And thus the secrets of his heart are revealed; and so, falling down on his face, he will worship God and report that God is truly among you."

Prophecy can reveal the secrets of an unbeliever's heart. It can confront the unbeliever with his or her sins; and, cause them to come to God asking for forgiveness and a clean heart. Verse 25 says that the unbeliever will gratefully fall down and worship.

Guidelines to Judging the Prophecy

1 Corinthians 14:29 (NKJV)

"Let two or three prophets speak, and let the others judge."

The Apostle Paul wrote 1 Corinthians 14:29 to address the issue of disorder in the local church at Corinth. He instructed the Corinthians to limit the number of people who would publicly prophesy at one time. He also established that it would be other prophets who would corroborate their words. These principles are valid today. We can apply them, not only to the context of corporate meetings, but also to individual choices we make about what has been spoken over us. (For the greatest safety, we should take the words of prophecy to be judged by a competent, seasoned spiritual authority.) The NIV translation of Verse 29 says, *"...weigh carefully what is said."* This brings us to the question of how we judge (or *"weigh carefully"*) prophecy?

We can begin to judge prophecy by discerning the intentions and character of the person who speaks it.

- Be careful whom you allow to speak into your life. Look to mature leaders to confirm the character of the person who is prophesying. Again, if you have doubts, bring your question to your leaders, who should be people of balanced, competent spiritual experience and authority. They will help you determine the truth.
- Be unwilling to listen to and receive a private word of prophecy. Ask the person who wants to give it to write it down or go with you to have it judged. If they will not, it is a safe and good practice to refuse to listen to it. Let your pastors and leaders protect you from false or carnal prophets. This is a dependable way to protect yourself.
- Never give a private word of prophecy, if you are unwilling to write it down and/or go to a spiritual authority and have it judged.

- Public prophecy is to be done decently and in order. Never receive or give prophecy that interrupts the flow of the Holy Spirit in a meeting. This is especially true when the Word of God is being preached.

Guidelines to Judge the Content of the Prophecy

1. DOES IT AGREE WITH THE WORD OF GOD?

Proverbs 30:5-6 (NKJV)

"Every word of God is pure; He is a shield to those who put their trust in Him. (6) Do not add to His words, Lest He rebuke you, and you be found a liar."

Titus 1:9 (NKJV)

"holding fast the faithful word as he has been taught, that he may be able, by sound doctrine, both to exhort and convict those who contradict."

2. DOES IT GLORIFY JESUS?

John 16:13-14 (NKJV)

"However, when He, the Spirit of truth, has come, He will guide you into all truth; for He will not speak on His own authority, but whatever He hears He will speak; and He will tell you things to come. {14} He will glorify Me, for He will take of what is Mine and declare it to you."

The Holy Spirit will let you know if it the prophecy is valid.

- He will guide you into all truth.

- He will not speak on His own authority.
- Whatever He hears from the Father He will speak.
- He will tell you things to come.
- He will take of what is Christ's and declare it to you. If it is authentic prophecy, it will glorify Christ!

Prophecy must do these things.
- Edify, encourage and comfort people.
- Build up the church.
- Profit people (be good for them).
- Bring the lost to repentance.
- Bear witness with your spirit.

Prophecy will never violate any of these things.

3. DOES THE PROPHECY BRING PEACE TO YOUR SPIRIT?

Peace in your spirit is the overriding quality by which you can judge whether a word of PROPHECY is from God. (Be aware that it may cause your flesh the opposite.)

Colossians 3:15 (NKJV)

"And let the peace of God rule in your hearts, to which also you were called in one body; and be thankful."

Guidelines to Prophesying

1 Corinthians 13:9 (NKJV)

"For we know in part and we prophesy in part."

Like a WORD OF KNOWLEDGE or WORD OF WISDOM, the gift of PROPHECY is spoken in part. It is not the whole picture.

If you are prophesying...

1. Do not try to interpret or explain what you have spoken. This is not your responsibility. In most cases, it is beyond your ability.

2. Do not expect to understand everything you say. You are not required by God to do this, nor are you able to do so.

3. Do not keep talking when God has finished. This is an easy mistake to make. Fear of man or inexperience will cause this. Remember, it takes practice to hear from God.

4. Do not be a "parking lot" or "curbside prophet." Do not ambush people outside the church (or anywhere else) to give them a word (Do not allow others to do this to you.)

Questions for Discussion

1. How would you explain the differences between *"edification," "exhortation," and comfort"* as they are used in the Bible? Can you give examples in the context of your life today?

2. What other spiritual gifts would you turn to when trying to judge a prophecy someone is giving?

3. What is the greatest barrier to accepting prophecy as something the Holy Spirit still does today?

FOURTEEN

The Three Vocal/Utterance Gifts... for You

1 Corinthians 12:10b (NKJV)

"...to another prophecy, to another discerning of spirits, to another different kinds of tongues, to another the interpretation of tongues."

Second Vocal/Utterance Gift:
DIFFERENT KINDS OF TONGUES

Two sets of thoughts provide a clear definition of the gift of tongues: *"The gift of tongues is "an ability given spontaneously by the Holy Spirit to an individual to speak in a language unknown to the speaker"...It can be exercised and expanded."*[25] *"The realm in which the gift of tongues operates is not the human mind.... The mind is primarily a spectator to the events, and it neither frames the utterances, nor does it premeditate or arrange them."*[26]

Tongues are the Initial Evidence of the Baptism in the Holy Spirit.

The events preceding, and on the Day of Pentecost form the New Testament pattern for the baptism in the Holy Spirit.

[25] Clinton, Spiritual Gifts, P.65-66.
[26] Holbrook, The Holy Spirit, P.161.

151

Acts 1:4-5 (NKJV)

"And being assembled together with them, He commanded them not to depart from Jerusalem, but to wait for the Promise of the Father, "which," He said, "you have heard from Me; {5} for John truly baptized with water, but you shall be baptized with the Holy Spirit not many days from now."

Acts 2:1-4 (NKJV)

"When the Day of Pentecost had fully come, they were all with one accord in one place. {2} And suddenly there came a sound from heaven, as of a rushing mighty wind, and it filled the whole house where they were sitting. {3} Then there appeared to them divided tongues, as of fire, and one sat upon each of them. {4} And they were all filled with the Holy Spirit and began to speak with other tongues, as the Spirit gave them utterance."

Today, the testimony or an evidence of the baptism in the Holy Spirit remains that the Spirit-baptized believer speaks in unrecognizable *"other tongues."* There are many other evidences in a believer's life, but the gift of DIFFERENT KINDS OF TONGUES is the initial evidence of the baptism in the Holy Spirit. In the Book of Acts, there are at least three instances of believers being baptized in the Holy Spirit, and then speaking in tongues.

1. Acts 2:1-4

2. Acts 10:44-46

3. Acts 19:1-6

Some believe that speaking in tongues will always occur at the instant of Spirit baptism. However, many experience delays (hours, weeks or even months) before this initial evidence manifests. For some, there may be barriers to speaking in tongues that must be broken. Some of these are fear, unbelief, misunderstanding, feelings of unworthiness, lack of knowledge, etc. We must be careful not judge anyone's commitment or walk with God by whether they speak in tongues.

Exercising the gift of DIFFERENT KINDS OF TONGUES is a great way for a believer to pray and worship. Kenneth Hagin says, *"This utterance gift of tongues is an important gift in that tongues is the door to the supernatural."*[27] Tongues are not the only door to communion with God, but they are a door that is always open and inviting. Tongues are supernatural in their qualities. They give a depth of prayer and worship that charismatic believers find to be priceless.

DIFFERENT KINDS OF TONGUES are a Great Gift When Privately Spoken.

Privately speaking in tongues is an expression of spiritual sacrifice. It sends this message: *"God, I want to be close to You. I want to remind myself to communicate with you. You are most important to me, regardless of what I am doing any time of the day or night."*

Speaking in tongues allow us to pray continuously, even when we have no words to express our hearts to God. The

---

[27] Hagin, The Holy Spirit and His Gifts, P.149.

Bible tells us, in 1 Thessalonians 5:17, that we may *"pray without ceasing."* This means that we may speak in tongues throughout the day, anywhere we are and regardless of what we are doing.

When we do not know how to pray about a particular need or situation, the Holy Spirit does the praying through us, as we pray in tongues. Then, we can be confident of perfect prayers.

Romans 8:26 (NKJV)

"Likewise the Spirit also helps in our weaknesses. For we do not know what we should pray for as we ought, but the Spirit Himself makes intercession for us with groanings which cannot be uttered."

Public Use of DIFFERENT KINDS OF TONGUES

(A Study from 1 Corinthians, Chapter 14)

When used in private, the gift of DIFFERENT KINDS OF TONGUES is for personal edification. When spoken in public, it should be for the profit (or good) of those listening. This requires that it be interpreted. Verses 6-11 of 1 Corinthians 14 explain that the gift of DIFFERENT KINDS OF TONGUES has four applications for public ministry. Each contains a communication directly from God. Each has specific conditions that allow this gift to be applicable in public.

1 Corinthians 14:6-11 (NKJV)

"But now, brethren, if I come to you speaking with tongues, what shall I profit you unless I speak to

you either by revelation, by knowledge, by prophesying, or by teaching? {7} Even things without life, whether flute or harp, when they make a sound, unless they make a distinction in the sounds, how will it be known what is piped or played? {8} For if the trumpet makes an uncertain sound, who will prepare himself for battle? {9} So likewise you, unless you utter by the tongue words easy to understand, how will it be known what is spoken? For you will be speaking into the air. {10} There are, it may be, so many kinds of languages in the world, and none of them is without significance. {11} Therefore, if I do not know the meaning of the language, I shall be a foreigner to him who speaks, and he who speaks will be a foreigner to me."

Here are four applications of the gift of DIFFERENT KINDS OF TONGUES: (1) to provide revelation; (2) to give knowledge and understanding from God; (3) to work together with PROPHECY; and, (4) to teach. A fifth application, that it is a sign to unbelievers, is found in 1 Corinthians 14:22.

1 Corinthians 14:22 (NKJV)

"Therefore tongues are for a sign, not to those who believe but to unbelievers..."

We are given further instructions in 1 Corinthians, Chapter 14 concerning speaking the gift of DIFFERENT KINDS OF TONGUES in public.

1 Corinthians 14:5 (NKJV)

"I wish you all spoke with tongues, but even more that you prophesied; for he who prophesies is greater than he who speaks with tongues, unless indeed he interprets, that the church may receive edification."

1 Corinthians 14:18-23 (NKJV)

"I thank my God I speak with tongues more than you all; {19} yet in the church I would rather speak five words with my understanding, that I may teach others also, than ten thousand words in a tongue.

Paul cautioned the Corinthians not to abuse the gift of DIFFERENT KINDS OF TONGUES by speaking them in ways that were out of order. Without the gift of INTERPRETATION OF TONGUES there is no understandable communication between the person speaking and others who may be listening. The listeners are not edified. Paul said that he wished all believers spoke in tongues, but he qualified this by saying that publicly speaking in tongues ought to be interpreted. Again, this is because their interpretation will edify the body of Christ. In 1 Corinthians 14:16, Paul wrote, *"...how will he who occupies the place of the uninformed say "Amen" at your giving of thanks, since he does not understand what you say?"* Remember that edification is the primary purpose of the nine gifts of the Holy Spirit. We will look at the gift of INTERPRETATION OF TONGUES next.

Third Vocal/Utterance Gift:
INTERPRETATION OF TONGUES

INTERPRETATION OF TONGUES is the only one of the nine gifts of the Holy Spirit, listed in 1 Corinthians 12, that depends completely on one of the other gifts. It cannot operate on its own. Some of the other nine gifts work together with each other, but this gift depends completely on the manifestation of the gift of TONGUES. The purpose of INTERPRETATION OF TONGUES is solely to make known what has been uttered by someone publicly speaking in tongues. Those who hear the interpretation will then understand what the Holy Spirit is saying.[28]

INTERPRETATION OF TONGUES in Public Ministry

1 Corinthians 14:27 (NKJV)

"If anyone speaks in a tongue, let there be two or at the most three, each in turn, and let one interpret."

Paul knew that the Corinthians had improper excesses in their public ministry. There was much confusion from everyone shouting out messages in tongues during a service. Without orderly interpretation, there was chaos in the congregation. This needed to be corrected. These excesses were bringing disunity and discord. In 1 Corinthians 14:27, Paul wrote that two or three may speak publicly in tongues. Then, one person should interpret in an orderly fashion. These instructions provide the effect of maintaining order.

---

[28] 1 Corinthians 14:4-5.

Paul originally gave his instructions to address a problem in the Corinthian church two millennia ago, in their local time and place. Are Paul's instructions to the Corinthians on the interpretation of tongues valid for us today? The answer to this question of validity is found in the literary context of all of Chapter 12, which confirms that Paul's instructions to the Corinthian church on the interpretation of tongues are "normative"[29] for today. Nowhere in Chapter 12 are Paul's instructions expressly limited to that one particular occasion and time (as parts of other chapters, such as Chapter 14, may be[30]). They have dual applications, first locally and then universally.

The local pastor, or ministry leader, who is the spiritual authority of the meeting, will determine the details and set the rules for how tongues and interpretation are to flow in the meeting, or even if they will be allowed. Whether we may agree or disagree with these rules, we are subject to spiritual authority and must release our opinions to God. In every case, spiritual authority is to be delegated from the Senior Pastor or Senior Ministry Leader to their local leaders.

The interpretation of the message in tongues may be given by the person speaking the tongue. However, another may follow the utterance of the tongues with its interpretation. When more than one person tries to interpret the same utterance, and there is confusion or what seems like a

---

[29] To be normative is to be accepted as normal in a culture, time and place.
[30] An example of scriptural instruction concerning a locally isolated problem is found in 1 Corinthians 14:34-35, which addressed the immediate problem of unruly, rebellious women in that particular church.

disconnect, it is a signal to be cautious about what you receive. Confusion or a disconnect occur for a variety of reasons. These may include inexperience with the gift, or a carnal desire to influence the listeners, through the interpretation of the tongues. God is not confused, nor is His word to us.

1 Corinthians 14:33, 40 (NKJV)

"For God is not the author of confusion but of peace, as in all the churches of the saints... Let all things be done decently and in order."

Judging the Interpretation

When we are consistently walking with the Lord, we have the capacity to judge whether the interpretation of the tongues is proper. Our measuring rod comes with our ability to discern whether the interpretation edifies the people to whom it is spoken. Edification is the key. Remember that to edify is to bring someone closer to God, and to build them up, as they are encouraged to move ahead in the will of God. This may be done in many ways. It sometimes includes a word of correction or even a rebuke that the Holy Spirit delivers through the interpretation of the tongues. Edification is not about feelings. It is always about speaking words that direct God's people to walk on a righteous path.

Proverbs 4:18-19 (NIV)

"The path of the righteous is like the first gleam of dawn, shining ever brighter till the full light of day. But the way of the wicked is like deep

159

darkness; they do not know what makes them stumble.

Every word spoken during the interpretation of the tongues is meant by the Holy Spirit to bring opportunities for the hearer(s) to act upon it and draw nearer to God. If the words spoken are of God and people find them difficult to accept, this usually means the message has been provided to correct their paths and steer them from dark to light.

It is vital to be listening in the spirit and not the flesh. This will help us not to be led astray by a false interpretation. Remember, only the Holy Spirit can witness to us whether the interpretation is correct. We must walk humbly before Him with fear and reverence, so we can clearly discern His witness of the truthfulness of the interpretation.

Romans 8:5 (NKJV)

"For those who live according to the flesh set their minds on the things of the flesh, but those who live according to the Spirit, the things of the Spirit."

Interpretation is Not Translation.

There is a difference between interpretation and translation.
- Interpretation is a paraphrase of what has been spoken, for the purpose of making its meaning clear. It may be imperfect and incomplete. When we exercise the gift of interpretation from 1 Corinthians 12:10, it always requires input from the Holy Spirit. It cannot be done without Him.

- Translation is an attempt at an exact representation in a second language of what has been said. Translation, like interpretation, may also be imperfect and incomplete. However, it is solely a naturally acquired and demonstrated skill. It does not depend on input from the Holy Spirit.
- The use of THE GIFT OF INTERPRETATION OF TONGUES is never a literal representation or translation of what was spoken. The interpreter uses his or her spiritual gift to interpret (as with a paraphrase), not to translate.
- The interpretation may be considerably longer or shorter than the utterance. Do not try to compare the length of the utterance to the length of the interpretation. Doing this will mislead you and may cause you to reject what God has spoken.
- Remember that the interpretation is spoken as part of the message. Remember also, that in most cases, the interpreter cannot explain the interpretation. The interpretation ought to be between you and the Holy Spirit. Therefore, if you give the interpretation of a message in tongues, do not feel pressured or obligated to explain or remember what you said.

Private Devotions and Prayers

There are times when the gift of INTERPRETATION OF TONGUES is intended for private, personal devotions. We speak in tongues without any idea of what we have said. However, God may want us to know what the Holy Spirit said when we spoke in tongues. He may also want us to know what we said to God in our tongues. It is at times like these that God will allow us to interpret our own prayer language.

Conclusion to Part Two: The Nine Gifts of the Holy Spirit... For You

We have studied all nine gifts of the Spirit. First, we learned about the three Revelation Gifts. These gifts are given to reveal something supernatural (WORD OF WISDOM, WORD OF KNOWLEDGE and DISCERNING OF SPIRITS). Then we studied the three power gifts (FAITH, GIFTS OF HEALINGS and WORKING OF MIRACLES). These gifts are given for us to be the vessels that God uses to do something supernatural. Finally, we have studied the three vocal/utterance gifts (PROPHECY, TONGUES and INTERPRETATION OF TONGUES). These gifts are given so that we might say something supernatural, straight from the throne of Almighty God.

Through these nine gifts of the Holy Spirit from 1 Corinthians, Chapter 12, God provided all we need to speak of the victorious Christian life to our brothers and sisters. Ask God for your gift. He will never give you a stone!

Luke 11:11-13 (NKJV)

"If a son asks for bread from any father among you, will he give him a stone? Or if he asks for a fish, will he give him a serpent instead of a fish? {12} Or if he asks for an egg, will he offer him a scorpion? {13} If you then, being evil, know how to give good gifts to your children, how much more will your heavenly Father give the Holy Spirit to those who ask Him!"

Questions for Discussion

1. Does it make sense to you that when the interpretation is spoken, it might be of a very different length then the original tongues? Why does it usually need to be a different length?

2. Very few subjects evoke more emotion and controversy in the Body of Christ than whether the nine gifts of the Spirit are still in operation today. Your opinion probably depends on the doctrines you have accepted as normative for today.
   - Why would you argue that all nine gifts of the Spirit from 1 Corinthians, Chapter 12 are necessary for someone to walk in the fullness of the Holy Spirit?
   - If you do not believe they are normative today, on what would you scripturally base your belief?[31]

3. What do you think are (or were in biblical times) the most common abuses of the nine gifts of the Holy Spirit? List three if you can.

   (1)
   (2)
   (3)

4. What do you think are (or were in biblical times) the most common blessings that come from these nine gifts?

---

[31] Be assured that I (Dr. Abramson) do not accept that our brothers and sisters, whose doctrines do not teach that these nine gifts are normative today, are any less spiritual than those of us who embrace them as gifts for us to use today. To do so would be prideful and full of judgment. We all have enough trouble with these works of the flesh without directing them toward our brothers and sisters in Christ. Let the Spirit of Grace rule your heart and mind.

Part Three: The Holy Spirit… With You

FIFTEEN

Another Comforter, Helper, Counselor

John 14:16-17

King James Version (KJV)

"And I will pray the Father, and he shall give you another Comforter, that he may abide with you for ever; {17} Even the Spirit of truth; whom the world cannot receive, because it seeth him not, neither knoweth him: but ye know him; for he dwelleth with you, and shall be in you."

New King James Version (NKJV)

"And I will pray the Father, and He will give you another Helper, that He may abide with you forever; {17} the Spirit of truth, whom the world cannot receive, because it neither sees Him nor knows Him; but you know Him, for He dwells with you and will be in you."

New International Version (NIV)

"And I will ask the Father, and he will give you another Counselor to be with you forever-- {17} the Spirit of truth. The world cannot accept him, because it neither sees him nor knows him. But

you know him, for he lives with you and will be in you."

The original Greek word for *"Comforter"* is *"parakletos."*[32] As you have seen from the three translations above. *"parakletos"* has been translated as *"Comforter," "Helper,"* and *"Counselor."*

It is clear that the biblical synonyms for *"parakletos"* all describe the Holy Spirit's presence and functions as edifying, encouraging and uplifting. Whatever we need is available as we turn to Him and seek His aid for our needs at a particular moment.

- The Holy Spirit brings us comfort when we are uncomfortable or upset over of our circumstances.
- He is available to help when we are in situations that we cannot cope with and need His divine intervention.
- He brings us counsel that is always correct, complete and capable of taking us through whatever we are unsure of. Because He is perfect, and therefore His counsel and ways are perfect, He will never fail us. For the person that understands this, it becomes a reflex action to trust Him in the midst of anything.

Strong's Dictionary also adds *"intercessor"* and *"advocate"* to define the word *"parakletos."*[33] The Holy Spirit is always available to intercede for us. He prays to the Father when we do not know how to pray.

---

[32] Strong's Number 3875.
[33] ibid.

"Likewise the Spirit also helps in our weaknesses. For we do not know what we should pray for as we ought, but the Spirit Himself makes intercession for us with groanings which cannot be uttered. {27} Now He who searches the hearts knows what the mind of the Spirit is, because He makes intercession for the saints according to the will of God."

The Holy Spirit prays perfect prayers that meet the need of the moment. As He prays, Jesus receives, agrees with, and presents His prayers to the Father. The Holy Spirit, as a member of the divine Trinity, always functions in complete agreement with Christ and the Father.

Another Comforter Just Like Jesus

Following His death, burial, resurrection and ascension, Jesus sent the Holy Spirit to fill the void that was left when He went to the Father. We know that the Holy Spirit is not a copy of Jesus. He is unique, and uniquely the Third Person of the Trinity. He is not God's Son, nor is He the Father. So, what makes Him *"another Comforter"* or *"Helper"* or *"Counselor"* just like Jesus? The answer is found in the Holy Spirit's attributes. Attributes are the qualities or characteristics of a person. What makes the Holy Spirit just like Jesus is that they share common attributes within their hearts. The following are some of these attributes. Each will provide you with insight into how the Holy Spirit is *"another Comforter"* just like Jesus.

The three translations with which we began the chapter describe the Holy Spirit as, *"another Comforter, another Helper,"* and *"another Counselor."* Let's look further at these three descriptions of how He functions:

1. *"COMFORTER"* (KJV)

One of Jesus' primary functions in His earthly ministry was bring comfort and assurance in the midst of trials, uncertainties or other discomforting situations. He remains our good Shepherd. He still watches over us, in cooperation with the Holy Spirit; and, brings comfort as only a caring Shepherd can. Jesus sent the Holy Spirit to be His replacement when He ascended to Heaven. The Holy Spirit, though unique in His identity as a divine Person, shares the identical desire and ability to comfort us. Jesus said the Holy Spirit would abide with us forever. Comfort is only a heartbeat away. The New Living Translation puts it this way:

John 14:26-27 (KJV)

"But the Comforter, which is the Holy Ghost, whom the Father will send in my name, he shall teach you all things, and bring all things to your remembrance, whatsoever I have said unto you. {27} Peace I leave with you, my peace I give unto you: not as the world giveth, give I unto you. Let not your heart be troubled, neither let it be afraid."

2. "HELPER" (NKJV)

John 16:7 (NKJV)

"Nevertheless I tell you the truth. It is to your advantage that I go away; for if I do not go away, the Helper will not come to you; but if I depart, I will send Him to you."

God intends us to be capable of doing what our faith demands of us, especially in times of extreme challenge or testing. The Holy Spirit was sent to equip us to do what is required for each moment's victory or success. When we find it is beyond our human abilities, the Holy Spirit will intercede and provide what we cannot. (These are the moments our faith should arise; and, we should expect Him to be there for us and with us.) He is able to do whatever is necessary, as He works through us. With Him, all things are possible to the person who believes.

Ephesians 3:20 (NKJV)

"Now to Him who is able to do exceedingly abundantly above all that we ask or think, according to the power that works in us,"

Mark 9:23 (NKJV)

"Jesus said to him, "If you can believe, all things are possible to him who believes.""

3. *"Counselor"* (NIV)

John 16:13-15 (NIV)

"But when he, the Spirit of truth, comes, he will guide you into all truth. He will not speak on his own; he will speak only what he hears, and he will tell you what is yet to come. {14} He will bring glory to me by taking from what is mine and making it known to you. {15} All that belongs to the Father is mine. That is why I said the Spirit will take from what is mine and make it known to you."

John 16:13 reveals that the Holy Spirit is our Guide. He is with us as our *"Counselor."* He guides us into the truth from God. Therefore, when we accept His guidance, we are in agreement with the Godhead. This brings the assurance that what we receive from the Holy Spirit are principles and instructions for true success. Again, this is where our trust in Him is required, as we act upon what He says. The results, according to Jesus' own words, will glorify Him, as our Lord. This happens because we have acted with God-given wisdom and spiritual understanding. We gained this by listening to and obeying the voice of the Holy Spirit. What could be more assuring than to know that we have the Holy Spirit to provide us with counsel in every situation life's circumstances will bring us!

The Holy Spirit is your Comforter, Helper and Counselor. He is always there for you and will be with you. I encourage you to develop your relationship with Him. His heart's desire is to be closer to you. He is there to help you walk through every day of your life, so that you may reach and fulfill your destiny.

Questions for Discussion

1. What do you think are the most important attributes of the Holy Spirit, as they relate to your own purpose and journey through life?

2. We know we are to imitate Christ, through the power of the Holy Spirit. What limits you today from any particular attributes of His you ought to try to imitate?

SIXTEEN

A Journey of Your Choosing

Psalms 31:3 (NKJV)

"For You are my rock and my fortress; Therefore, for Your name's sake, Lead me and guide me."

Psalms 143:10 (NKJV)

"Teach me to do Your will, For You are my God; Your Spirit is good. Lead me in the land of uprightness."

Psalms 143:10 (NLT)

"Teach me to do your will, for you are my God. May your gracious Spirit lead me forward on a firm footing."

Let's begin with the same thought with which we ended the previous chapter: "What could be more assuring than to know that we have the Holy Spirit to provide us with counsel in every situation life's circumstances will bring us!" This thought holds within it, a guarantee from God. If you seek to have the Holy Spirit with you, as a habitual pattern in life, He will guide you past all the circumstances that may hinder your success. Be assured that the Holy Spirit will honor your desire and efforts to include Him in your daily walk. If you seek Him each morning, His unending faithfulness, in perfect agreement with the Father and Son, will be there for you. He is fully dependable. He will respond faithfully to your needs, as you walk through life with Him. This is a pattern the Godhead established in eternity past for all God's children who call Jesus their Lord; and, have chosen consistently to be *"guided by God's Spirit."*

Romans 8:14 (GWT)

"Certainly, all who are guided by God's Spirit are God's children."

Romans 8:14 (ICB)

"The true children of God are those who let God's Spirit lead them."

There is a difference between involuntarily being pushed (or driven) and choosing to be led. The Holy Spirit's great pleasure is to be with you every day, leading your every step. However, He will not force you to include Him in your life, or force-feed you with demands to walk with Him. Because the Holy Spirit has a great love for you, He will wait for you to invite Him to lead you. It will be your daily choice to include Him. Never forget His compassion and faithfulness. *"They are new every morning."* Why would you want to go through any day without Him?

Lamentations 3:22-23 (NIV)

"Because of the Lord's great love we are not consumed, for his compassions never fail. {23} They are new every morning; great is your faithfulness."

176

I am sure you are aware that you will not be able to dictate all the circumstances of your journey through life. However, let me assure you that you will be the deciding factor in your attitudes, as you walk through those circumstances. Either you will walk alone, or if you choose, you will benefit from the presence and guidance of the Holy Spirit. Romans 8:5-10 provides us with some contrasting characteristics of a life's journey, with or without the guidance of the Holy Spirit. The Scriptures clearly demonstrate that the fullness of the Holy Spirit in your life will depend on the choices you make to define your journey.

Romans 8:5-10 (NKJV)

"For those who live according to the flesh set their minds on the things of the flesh, but those who live according to the Spirit, the things of the Spirit. {6} For to be carnally minded is death, but to be spiritually minded is life and peace. {7} Because the carnal mind is enmity against God; for it is not subject to the law of God, nor indeed can be. {8} So then, those who are in the flesh cannot please God. {9} But you are not in the flesh but in the Spirit, if indeed the Spirit of God dwells in you. Now if anyone does not have the Spirit of Christ, he is not His. {10} And if Christ is in you, the body is dead because of sin, but the Spirit is life because of righteousness."

Life's Journey - What will You Choose?		
Verse	Walking by Yourself ("carnally minded")	Being Led by the Spirit ("spiritually minded")
{5}	Carnal thinking	Spiritually-led thinking
{6}	Death to your dreams, goals... and little effectiveness as a force for the Gospel	"...life and peace," including the ability to bring these two great blessings to others
{7}	"...not subject to the law of God"	
{8}	"...cannot please God"	
{9}		a. "...in the Spirit" b. "...the Spirit of God dwells in you."
{10}	Your body will remain carnal because of sin.	Your spirit will be alive, filled with the presence of Christ's righteousness.

As you can see from above, the choices you make on a daily basis will define your journey through life. The Apostle Paul provided us with some additional advantages of choosing the Holy Spirit as our walking Companion on a daily basis. These advantages will all assist in leading you into the fullness of your walk with the Holy Spirit. We also find them in Romans, Chapter 8.

Romans 8:26-32 (NKJV)

"Likewise the Spirit also helps in our weaknesses.

178

For we do not know what we should pray for as we ought, but the Spirit Himself makes intercession for us with groanings which cannot be uttered. {27} Now He who searches the hearts knows what the mind of the Spirit is, because He makes intercession for the saints according to the will of God. {28} And we know that all things work together for good to those who love God, to those who are the called according to His purpose. {29} For whom He foreknew, He also predestined to be conformed to the image of His Son, that He might be the firstborn among many brethren. {30} Moreover whom He predestined, these He also called; whom He called, these He also justified; and whom He justified, these He also glorified. {31} What then shall we say to these things? If God is for us, who can be against us? {32} He who did not spare His own Son, but delivered Him up for us all, how shall He not with Him also freely give us all things?"

Additional Advantages from Romans, Chapter 8

Verse 26: When the Holy Spirit is your daily walking Partner, He will be in constant intercession for you, especially in the midst of any confusion or doubt concerning your situation. Choose to rely completely on Him.

Verse 27: The Holy Spirit's intercession will be warmly received and acted upon in heaven, because it is the will of God.

Verse 28: When the Holy Spirit is your daily walking Partner, even what seems to be negative can come to a positive outcome. This happens because all things work together for good, when you are walking with the Holy Spirit, and have heaven's purposes in your heart.

Verse 29: Walk with the Holy Spirit on a daily basis and you will begin to look just a little bit more like Jesus every day. You will increasingly think like, speak like and love like Jesus. This is part of His divine plan for you. All it requires is that you understand its value and walk in it.

Verse 30: You will have the advantage of being *"justified"* and *"glorified."* These theological terms simply describe the following:

- To be justified is to gain God's declaration of righteousness, through your faith in Christ. God justifies you by declaring He will not blame you for your sins, because Jesus took the blame on the cross. You are declared to be entitled to the advantages and rewards that come from obedience to God's righteous requirements. Although your salvation brings immediate justification, your willingness to include the Holy Spirit in your daily walk builds on this and opens the gates to all its benefits.
- To be glorified means to be "ultimately and completely conformed to the image of Christ Jesus... It is the final link in the great golden chain of salvation. The apostle Paul refers to it as having already happened (Romans 8:30)."[34] "J.B. Philips says, God lifted them to the splendor of life as His own sons."[35]

---

[34] www.abide in Christ.com/selah/aug7.
[35] ibid. Quotes are in the public domain.

Verse 31: He will be with you and for you in your daily experiences, good or bad. Consider what an advantage this will be, on a day-by-day basis.

Verse 32: God has many good things that He desires to give to you. The Father, with Christ, will respond to the Holy Spirit's daily walk with you; and, move on behalf of His intercession for you. Your life's journey will be an experience in which you find so many good and precious gifts from God.

The list of advantages you have from choosing daily to walk with the Holy Spirit is never-ending. As the text in Romans, Chapter 8 concludes, Paul provides us with even more assurances of the benefits of walking with the Holy Spirit daily.

Romans 8:35-39 (NKJV)

"Who shall separate us from the love of Christ? Shall tribulation, or distress, or persecution, or famine, or nakedness, or peril, or sword? {36} As it is written: "For Your sake we are killed all day long; We are accounted as sheep for the slaughter." {37} Yet in all these things we are more than conquerors through Him who loved us. {38} For I am persuaded that neither death nor life, nor angels nor principalities nor powers, nor things present nor things to come, {39} nor height nor depth, nor any other created thing, shall be able to separate us from the love of God which is in Christ Jesus our Lord."

Verse 35: All the negative, potentially destructive things that try to come between you and Christ will fail, because your daily walk with the Holy Spirit will strengthen you in your relationship with Him, and therefore, with Christ.

Verse 37: You are more than a conqueror through the power of the Holy Spirit, as He works with the same love that the Father and Christ have bestowed on you. Stay close to the Holy Spirit. Include Him in your daily decisions and He will take you to your victories.

Verses 38-39: these final two verses elaborate on Verse 35. In them, Paul provided a comprehensive list of those negative things that might try to separate you from God's love in Christ. Paul wrote this to emphasize how powerfully unbreakable the bond with God is for those who walk closely with the Holy Spirit. Ultimately, this bond is nothing less than the love of God, itself. I Corinthians 13:8 tells us that this bond (God's kind of love) never fails. It is eternal.

You have just read a lengthy list of your advantages, as a Christian who walks in a close relationship with the Holy Spirit, and who wisely makes your decisions with His counsel. Do your best and God will do the rest. Be committed to as full a relationship with the Holy Spirit as you can. It will lead you to enjoy the fullness of His Spirit in you, for you and with you.

Questions for Discussion

1. Take a few minutes now to reflect on what gives you comfort in the midst of discomforting circumstances? After you have done so, how much of what you reflected upon includes the Holy Spirit? Where do you think He should have more influence in determining your comfort level?

2. Should knowing the will of God for you life ever cause you discomfort? Think about this question carefully and then consider what God's Word tells you. Here are three verses of Scripture that you might want to study before you attempts to answer this question:

Romans 8:27-29 (NKJV)

"Now He who searches the hearts knows what the mind of the Spirit is, because He makes intercession for the saints according to the will of God. {28} And we know that all things work together for good to those who love God, to those who are the called according to His purpose. {29} For whom He foreknew, He also predestined to be conformed to the image of His Son, that He might be the firstborn among many brethren."

3. What personal value do you see in being *"conformed to the image of His Son"*?

4. In what circumstances would your natural inclination be to hold back from the process of being *"conformed"* to Christ's image? (Be transparent and honest with your answer.)

SEVENTEEN

A Demonstration of the Spirit and Power

1 Corinthians 2:1-5 (NKJV)

"And I, brethren, when I came to you, did not come with excellence of speech or of wisdom declaring to you the testimony of God. {2} For I determined not to know anything among you except Jesus Christ and Him crucified. {3} I was with you in weakness, in fear, and in much trembling. {4} And my speech and my preaching were not with persuasive words of human wisdom, but in demonstration of the Spirit and of power, {5} that your faith should not be in the wisdom of men but in the power of God."

Humility

Paul began 1 Corinthians, Chapter 2 with a declaration of his humble understanding of himself. He discounted his own speech and wisdom. He wrote that he did not come to his Corinthian brothers and sisters to declare Christ in the power of his own abilities or accomplished communication skills. He wrote this to remind them that it was Christ in Him, working through the Holy Spirit, who enabled Him to share what he had written to them. He took no glory in his esteemed position among the saints. Paul had seen Jesus. He had heard His voice. He knew that he was a sinner, saved by grace and called to be God's messenger of hope. All of this came from a man who was now operating in the fullness of the Holy Spirit; and, had power given to him to perform signs, wonders and miracles. It seemed that, instead of this power and privilege puffing him up with pride, it had given him a proper understanding of who he was in Christ. He was God's winner and champion, only because the Holy Spirit was there in him, for him and with him.

Concentrating on Jesus

1 Corinthians 2:2 (NKJV)

"For I determined not to know anything among you except Jesus Christ and Him crucified."

1 Corinthians 2:2 (NLT)

"For I decided to concentrate only on Jesus Christ and his death on the cross."

Paul continued with his writing by reminding the Corinthians that, while he was among them, he was focused completely on Christ and His atoning work on the cross. His message always led people to Jesus. It was primarily about how the Lord died for their sins (and ours), was buried and rose from the dead on the third day. Now, all believers would enjoy the fruits of Christ's atoning labor of sacrificial love. In testifying to this, Paul knew that he had to rely on the Holy Spirit. His demonstration had to be a display of spiritual wisdom in how he lived among the Corinthians, and especially in the ways he loved them. Paul would later remind them of this. The New Living Translation makes this reminder as clearly as it could be stated:

1 Corinthians 15:3-4 (NLT)

"I passed on to you what was most important and what had also been passed on to me--that Christ died for our sins, just as the Scriptures said. {4} He was buried, and he was raised from the dead on the third day, as the Scriptures said."

Paul did not justify what he had conveyed to the Corinthians by any argument except to direct them to Scripture. He understood that the ultimate power in his testimony lay in the Scriptures. Paul knew that, as the Corinthian church referred to the Scriptures and their oral traditions, they would have the anointing of the Holy Spirit to help them gain the wisdom and spiritual understanding necessary to grasp the enormity of their message.

Meekness is not Weakness.

1 Corinthians 2:3 (NKJV)

"I was with you in weakness, in fear, and in much trembling."

1 Corinthians 2:3 (NLT)

"I came to you in weakness--timid and trembling."

Paul, this giant of faith, was merely a human being who had his own weaknesses and fears. He was our example of someone with a humble spirit and desire to honor Christ. He relied on the Holy Spirit to help him deliver the message; and, do the work that he was called to do on behalf of the Lord. Can you see how God can use you, regardless of what you may or may not have right now as spiritual gifts? The Holy Spirit alone decides to whom, when and where He will give them. From his own experience, Here are Paul's words, concerning the Holy Spirit's giving of spiritual gifts:

1 Corinthians 12:11 (NLT)

"It is the one and only Holy Spirit who distributes these gifts. He alone decides which gift each person should have."

We should certainly ask the Holy Spirit for the spiritual gifts we seek. God's Word says that we ought to desire these gifts.[36] When we do, it is God's pleasure to give them to us, but they will always fit the Holy Spirit's plans for our lives.

A Distinctly Clear and Plain Message

1 Corinthians 2:4 (NKJV)

"And my message and my preaching were very plain. I did not use wise and persuasive speeches, but the Holy Spirit was powerful among you."

Paul was highly educated and came from the intensely religious background of a Pharisee. However, this religious training and its complicated way of thinking would be of limited value to him in presenting the Gospel. The salvation

---

[36] 1 Corinthians 14:1.

message he was now called to deliver was perfectly plain in its content. It was best served by a simple, non-religious sounding delivery. Paul had learned this through his earlier experiences with Christ and then with the church. When Paul delivered the Gospel, he did so expecting the power of the Holy Spirit to bring revelation, and therefore, radical transformation.

In this fourth verse, Paul testified that he felt powerless and ineffective in his natural ability to deliver the message. He had relied completely upon the Holy Spirit, who Paul knew to be majestic and all-powerful. This contrast helps us see that we have the unlimited potential to perform the will of God successfully, if we rely completely on Him. Effective delivery of the Gospel message ultimately depends on allowing the Holy Spirit to have control.

We can be assured that God will never send us alone, spiritually, into a situation in which we are to testify. The Holy Spirit will always be there with us. When it seems that we are in waters too deep to swim in, the Holy Spirit will keep us afloat and perform His will through us. This means that the apparent outcomes of our testimonies of Christ are not our responsibility. We are only accountable to speak plainly about the Lord. Then, we are to trust God for outcomes we may or may not ever see. They are the Holy Spirit's responsibility. (This reaffirms what Paul had written in Verse 2. He had committed to concentrating his efforts on the testimony of Christ.)

1 Corinthians 2:2 (NLT)

"For I decided to concentrate only on Jesus Christ and his death on the cross."

1 Corinthians 2:5 (NKJV)

"...that your faith should not be in the wisdom of men but in the power of God."

1 Corinthians 2:5 (NLT)

"I did this so that you might trust the power of God rather than human wisdom."

God is always concerned with who or what we allow to be master of our hearts. He saw the overwhelming motivation in Paul's heart was his commitment to be the bondservant of Christ. God also saw that Paul's concern for those he delivered the message to, was that they would take themselves beyond their natural thinking and into the realm of spiritual thinking... and a new, ever deepening spiritual relationship with Christ.

Romans 12:2 (NLT)

"Don't copy the behavior and customs of this world, but let God transform you into a new person by changing the way you think. Then you will know what God wants you to do, and you will know how good and pleasing and perfect his will really is."

Paul knew that when believers are led by and dependent on the Spirit of God, they find the peace that only comes from trusting Him. Then, they could follow their trust with their unwavering acceptance of His leading. This would result in them being able to do the will of God, regardless of the apparent barriers they faced. Doing the will of God, as they relied upon the Holy Spirit, would lead them to go far beyond natural wisdom and see things as God does. This would bring them along on the path God had preordained, which leads to success and significance in His kingdom.

Proverbs 4:18 (NLT)

"The way of the righteous is like the first gleam of dawn, which shines ever brighter until the full light of day."

Humility, meekness, trust and a clear, simple Gospel message are what God requires. As you have read in this chapter, anyone who has a heart to serve God can display these qualities and deliver the Gospel message with success. The Holy Spirit will be faithful to walk with you wherever He may send you. I encourage you to honor the great commission and be God's messenger.

Mark 10:27b (NKJV)

"...With men it is impossible, but not with God; for with God all things are possible."

Questions for Discussion

1. Humility, meekness, trust (and of course, belief) seem to be the foremost prerequisites for being God's Gospel delivery person. Which of these traits is weakest in you? How could you strengthen it? (Support your answer with Scripture.)

2. If meekness is not weakness, what is it? Why is having a spirit of meekness an advantage to God's servant, especially in the delivery of the Gospel? (If you do not think it is an advantage, explain why not.)

3. What would you say is the greatest barrier to others receiving the Gospel message?

4. Do you think anyone can receive the Gospel? Are there some people who are unable to do so? Explain which side of this argument you agree with.

EIGHTEEN
Revealed Through His Spirit

1 Corinthians 2:6-10 (NKJV)

"However, we speak wisdom among those who are mature, yet not the wisdom of this age, nor of the rulers of this age, who are coming to nothing. {7} But we speak the wisdom of God in a mystery, the hidden wisdom which God ordained before the ages for our glory, {8} which none of the rulers of this age knew; for had they known, they would not have crucified the Lord of glory {9} But as it is written: "Eye has not seen, nor ear heard, Nor have entered into the heart of man The things which God has prepared for those who love Him." {10} But God has revealed them to us through His Spirit. For the Spirit searches all things, yes, the deep things of God."

Not the Wisdom of This Age

On Page 96, I wrote the following:

"Do not waste an opportunity to ask God for what you need that will enable you to make a difference for others. Then, when the Lord provides it, be sure to use it wisely."

You read my brief analysis of Ephesians 1:16-20, in which I labeled these verses "A Prayer for Spiritual Wisdom and Understanding." You also came across these words on Page 52:

> "Without the Holy Spirit's direction, we cannot properly apply spiritual wisdom or understanding."

Now let's look at the Scriptures with which we started this chapter. They show us that Paul was concerned with the vital subject of the wisdom of God. (Indeed, it is a theme found in both Paul's writings and elsewhere in much of Scripture. We have both the New Testament and Old Testament wisdom literature to teach us about wisdom.) As you read in the previous chapter, Paul said that earthly wisdom was not what was required to share the Gospel. In 1 Corinthians 2:6-10, Paul then elaborated on the differences between spiritually sourced and naturally based wisdom. We will unpack Paul's thoughts as he continued with the next five verses (Verses 6-10).

Key Points to 1 Corinthians 2:6-10
(Not the Wisdom of This Age)
Verse

{6} *"However, we speak wisdom among those who are mature, yet not the wisdom of this age, nor of the rulers of this age, who are coming to nothing."*[37]

Paul used the word *"mature,"* to speak of people who were established in the faith and seasoned in the things

---

[37] Paul's use of the word *"However"* functioned as a connector to link the thoughts of Verse 6 to his thoughts in the previous five verses.

of God. The implication was that Paul expected the Corinthians to behave according to the level of maturity they should have had in their faith and fellowship with each other. It was distinctly opposite of what their culture in Corinth would have considered acceptable behavior. It was wisdom of the Kingdom of God.

{7} Paul continued the thought in Verse 6 with an explanation of what this wisdom was: *"But we speak the wisdom of God in a mystery, the hidden wisdom which God ordained before the ages for our glory,"*

Paul described this wisdom as contained *"in a mystery."* He used this term elsewhere in his writings as a metaphor for that which the Gospel makes available. It had not been revealed to everyone, but only to those who had a heart to receive it. This is still how it is today.

The Greek word translated, *"for our glory,"* is *"doxa."*[38] Paul intended it to have a wider application that would direct others to the magnificence of God. We can paraphrase this use of *"doxa"* as, *"for a display of the Gospel in our lives that signals the "dignity, honor, praise and worship" of Christ..."*

Paul saw this wisdom as established, or *"ordained"* by the Godhead even before the Word (Christ) created the heavens and earth. These thoughts were completed in Verse 8.

---

[38] Strong's Number G1391.

{8} *"...which none of the rulers of this age knew; for had they known, they would not have crucified the Lord of glory."*

Paul did not intend to excuse the behavior of the Lord's executioners. Those among them who never gave their lives to Christ would still face His ultimate judgment. Paul's point was that if anyone could see the Lord in all His glory, it should be a normal reaction that he or she would surrender immediately to His majestic person and presence. A reading of Revelation 19:11-16 makes this perfectly clear.

Revelation 19:11-16 (NKJV)

"Now I saw heaven opened, and behold, a white horse. And He who sat on him was called Faithful and True, and in righteousness He judges and makes war. {12} His eyes were like a flame of fire, and on His head were many crowns. He had a name written that no one knew except Himself. {13} He was clothed with a robe dipped in blood, and His name is called The Word of God. {14} And the armies in heaven, clothed in fine linen, white and clean, followed Him on white horses. {15} Now out of His mouth goes a sharp sword, that with it He should strike the nations. And He Himself will rule them with a rod of iron. He Himself treads the winepress of the fierceness and wrath of Almighty God. {16} And He has on His robe and on His thigh a name written: KING OF KINGS AND LORD OF LORDS."

{9} *"But as it is written: "Eye has not seen, nor ear heard, Nor have entered into the heart of man The things which God has prepared for those who love Him.""*

The preparation Paul referred to was, *"for those who love Him."* Here, Paul's reference was to *"things."* These are the blessings yet to be revealed to His church. This was a reference to the end of the age, that we read about in the final two chapters of Revelation. There, God declares from His throne, *"I make all things new."*[39] This is a statement of coming fact. It speaks to the church of God's promise for the future.

{10} *"But God has revealed them to us through His Spirit. For the Spirit searches all things, yes, the deep things of God."*

God has made known these *"things"* He has made preparation for His church *"through His Spirit."* It is God's will for us to know these *"things"* now. We find them out through an ever-closer relationship with the Holy Spirit. The stronger this relationship is, the more you will gain an intimate, faith-filled understand of these *"deep things."*

The Holy Spirit searches our unanswered questions, sees our needs and anticipates our purposes. Then, He reveals those things that can only be spoken Spirit to spirit. Can you see the decided advantage you will have if you are walking in the fullness of your relationship to the Holy Spirit?

---

[39] See Revelation 21:5.

Thus far, we have explored four topics in this final section, "Part Three: The Holy Spirit With You." These were: (1) "Another Comforter, Helper, Counselor;" (2) "A Journey of Your Choosing;" (3) "A Demonstration of the Spirit and Power;" and (4) "Revealed Through His Spirit." It is clear that the benefits of having the Holy Spirit with you are enormous. They should help you appreciate why this third section has been included in the book. I could not properly end without it. There are still two more chapters to complete. My prayer is that you will find the material I have presented to you as fuel to fire up the engine of faith within, as you gain an increase in spiritual wisdom and understanding. This would be an appropriate place to ask you again to read Paul's prayer in Colossians, Chapter 1. This time, I will present you with all five verses from the New Living Translation.

Colossians 1:9-14 (NLT)

"So we have continued praying for you ever since we first heard about you. We ask God to give you a complete understanding of what he wants to do in your lives, and we ask him to make you wise with spiritual wisdom. {10} Then the way you live will always honor and please the Lord, and you will continually do good, kind things for others. All the while, you will learn to know God better and better. {11} We also pray that you will be strengthened with his glorious power so that you will have all the patience and endurance you need. May you be filled with joy, {12} always thanking the Father, who has enabled you to

share the inheritance that belongs to God's holy people, who live in the light. {13} For he has rescued us from the one who rules in the kingdom of darkness, and he has brought us into the Kingdom of his dear Son. {14} God has purchased our freedom with his blood and has forgiven all our sins."

Read Verses 12-14 again. Then, think about the incredible gift they describe. As you do, thank God for His grace in your life. If you are living without Christ, ask Him to forgive you and be your Lord and Savior right now. Then, move on to the next two chapters, surrounded by His grace.

Questions for Discussion

1. In your own words, explain the difference between spiritually sourced and naturally based wisdom.

2. How does your current culture and environment improperly influence your thinking, when you should be relying on the wisdom of God's kingdom?

NINETEEN

Comparing Spiritual Things with Spiritual

1 Corinthians 2:11-13 (NKJV)

"For what man knows the things of a man except the spirit of the man which is in him? Even so no one knows the things of God except the Spirit of God. {12} Now we have received, not the spirit of the world, but the Spirit who is from God, that we might know the things that have been freely given to us by God. {13} These things we also speak, not in words which man's wisdom teaches but which the Holy Spirit teaches, comparing spiritual things with spiritual."

Let's move ahead with a discussion of some more key points to 1 Corinthians, Chapter 2. They will provide you with additional building blocks of understanding regarding your potential in Christ, and the possibilities within an increasingly full relationship with the Holy Spirit.

Key Points to 1 Corinthians 2:11-13
(Spirit to spirit)
Verse

{11} "For what man knows the things of a man except the spirit of the man which is in him? Even so no one

knows the things of God except the Spirit of God."

Paul used an easily understood comparison to remind his readers that the Holy Spirit is God and we are not. Therefore, as God, the Holy Spirit has unlimited access to all the depths of glory, inherent within the Godhead. The logical conclusion must be that without the Holy Spirit, we are captive to the need to rely upon only our natural thinking. With Him, we have access (as the Holy Spirit wills) to all the resources of heaven. You should find this both encouraging and motivating. Be encouraged that with God, all things are possible in your life. You can expect to go ever deeper in Him, if your heart desires to do so.

{12} *"Now we have received, not the spirit of the world, but the Spirit who is from God, that we might know the things that have been freely given to us by God."*

In this verse, Paul wrote of two things. First, he once again drew his readers' attention to the contrast between the world's spirit and the Spirit of God. Second, Paul's words were a statement of God's purpose. We have received the Holy Spirit so that we would not be ignorant of the divine resources He makes available to us. These are God's gifts. They are another indication of the vastness of His amazing grace in the life of the believer. Have you taken inventory lately of the grace in which you walk? Now would be an excellent time to do so. We all need to count our blessings as we remember that they are a function of God's grace, for which Jesus paid the ultimate price.

{13} These things we also speak, not in words which man's wisdom teaches but which the Holy Spirit teaches, comparing spiritual things with spiritual."

The *"things"* Paul wrote about in this verse finish his thought in Verse 12 - those *"freely given to us by God."* Paul suggested that we look at them through the lens of spirituality, that God freely provides us, comparing *"spiritual things with spiritual."* Here, once again, Paul has taken us back to the spiritual aspect of wisdom and understanding. He repeatedly drove home the point that we are born-again, spirit-filled beings and have the opportunity to live *"according to the Spirit"* (See again, Romans 8:1-5).

Paul was careful to turn his readers' attention back to the Holy Spirit. Paul took no credit for what he shared in his First Epistle to the Corinthians. Whatever they learned from Paul's words, was revealed and anointed by the Holy Spirit, who used His servant Paul to teach them. This may help you to accurately interpret and understand the meaning of what the Apostle John wrote in his First Epistle (and perhaps you can explain it to others, who have questions concerning the functions of the anointing).

1 John 2:27 (NKJV)

"But the anointing which you have received from Him abides in you, and you do not need that anyone teach you; but as the same anointing teaches you concerning all things, and is true, and is not a lie, and just as it has

taught you, you will abide in Him"

Now, we can move on to the next three verses of 1 Corinthians 2. We will continue to use the same format to analyze what Paul had written.

1 Corinthians 2:14-16 (NKJV)

"But the natural man does not receive the things of the Spirit of God, for they are foolishness to him; nor can he know them, because they are spiritually discerned. {15} But he who is spiritual judges all things, yet he himself is rightly judged by no one. {16} For "who has known the mind of the LORD that he may instruct Him?" But we have the mind of Christ."

Key Points to 1 Corinthians 2:14-16
(Spirit to spirit)

Verse

{14} *"But the natural man does not receive the things of the Spirit of God, for they are foolishness to him; nor can he know them, because they are spiritually discerned.*

Another way to accurately say what Paul has said in this verse is to paraphrase it as follows:

"However, neither the person who does not know Christ nor the Christian who is living a carnal life will receive the gift of God's wisdom. Because of their carnal thinking, God's wisdom would seem foolish. Therefore, the way these people are living restricts

them from knowing the things God. These things are not available to them. God cannot teach them to walk with Him in victory. This is because they are not wired into the ways God thinks and communicates."

Consider what undiscovered spiritual wisdom awaits any of us who do our best to walk in the fullness of the Holy Spirit. Every day we can go deeper in the things of God. Every day we can walk in greater spiritual wisdom and understanding. This is my prayer and desire each morning. Is it yours? If not, I encourage you to make it so, and begin to reap the benefits of your willingness to change. Be assured that the Holy Spirit will respond to your prayer.

{15} *"But he who is spiritual judges all things, yet he himself is rightly judged by no one."*

I have paraphrased this verse as follows:

"Once a believer in Christ has obediently submitted to the leading and teaching of the Holy Spirit (as a lifestyle), he or she has the spiritual equipment to understand every circumstance and situation. Words become open books. Actions will be viewed through that same spiritual lens that everyone who walks according to the Spirit has. The person who is spiritual may be judged by others, but in God's view, the others have no right to do so. This means he or she can stand on the platform of divine assurance, never falling into condemnation."

{16} *"For "who has known the mind of the LORD that he may instruct Him?" But we have the mind of Christ."*

205

To help understand how this verse fits with the previous one, I have provided the New Living Translation of both:

1 Corinthians 2:15-16 (NLT)

"We who have the Spirit understand these things, but others can't understand us at all. {16} How could they? For, "Who can know what the Lord is thinking? Who can give him counsel?" But we can understand these things, for we have the mind of Christ."

The final verse, which wraps up the translators' division of this chapter from the next one, reveals where Paul had been taking his readers. He ended the chapter by saying Christians can understand spiritual things because we have been given *"the mind of Christ."* This is a figure of speech and is not to be taken to mean we have the Lord's mind. Only God can have such a thing. What, then, did Paul mean?

Let's look more closely at two words in the expression, *"we have the mind of Christ."* The Greek word for *"have"* is *"echo."*[40] This implies that our thinking can replicate or project an image of what Christ is thinking. The second word, is *"mind."* The Greek word for *"mind"* is *"nous."* [41] This word may also be translated as *"understanding."* This leads to another of my paraphrases. Think about the

---

[40] Strong's number G2192.
[41] Strong's, number G1097.

expression *"we have the mind of Christ"* in this way:

"However, as Spirit-filled and Spirit-led believers, we can echo or present a like image of what Christ would think, because we understand and comprehend how He would see a particular circumstance or situation. Beyond this, we also have the ability to apply heaven's kind of reasoning to determine how we will react."

Every word Paul wrote in 1 Corinthians has the potential to lead us into seeing the value of an ever-deepening relationship with the Holy Spirit. As you process what you have read in this chapter and the others, I encourage you to hunger even more for the fullness of your relationship with the Holy Spirit. He has made it available to you. Now, let's proceed to the final chapter in the book.

Questions for Discussion

1. If you were to explain the term, "carnal Christian," what would you say? (Be careful not to be judgmental.)

2. 1 John 2:27 speaks of *"the anointing"* teaching us. How can this happen? Can you explain it in simple terms?

3. After reading 1 Corinthians 2:15-16 (NLT), can you explain what *"the mind of Christ"* means in terms an unbeliever would readily find understandable? (Do so without relying on my exact words or phrasing.)

4. This is the final question in the book. Now that you have finished nineteen chapters, can you explain, in your own

words, what the fullness of a relationship with the Holy Spirit means to you?

TWENTY

Blessed with the Spirit... For a Purpose

Throughout the preceding nineteen chapters, you have read many things about what the fullness of a relationship with the Holy Spirit can mean. I have written to you about the experience of having the fullness of the Holy Spirit "In You." Then, I wrote of His nine spiritual gifts, described in 1 Corinthians 12, working "For You." Now, in this section, I have written about having the Holy Spirit "With You." I would like to finish what I have to share by emphasizing how all these things are blessings; but more importantly, how they are part of a developing, intimate relationship with the Holy Spirit. That is the greatest blessing.

The Lord Jesus Christ made a great promise, which gives us assurance that we will never be alone. He said this about the Holy Spirit:

John 14:17 (NLT)

"He is the Holy Spirit, who leads into all truth. The world at large cannot receive him, because it isn't looking for him and doesn't recognize him. But you do, because he lives with you now and later will be in you."

The promise is clear. Jesus said that the Holy Spirit *"lives with you now and later will be in you."* Jesus was not restricting His promise to that particular occasion or culture in biblical Israel. It was, indeed, a promise for the ages. It extends to the citizens of the Kingdom of God in all places, for all times and in every occasion. I cannot think of any greater assurance.

I have emphasized throughout the book that the degree of intimacy we have with the Holy Spirit is conditional on our willingness to put forth the effort to draw near to Him and stay connected. If you understand who He is, this is not really asking anything difficult. It should be the most attractive and worthwhile condition that any of us could imagine. Here is the Spirit of God, in complete agreement with our heavenly Father and our Lord and Savior, Jesus Christ, extending the hand of close relationship... to you! Will you take His hand and hold on tightly, through thick and thin, good and bad, as a personal pattern of living? This is, in the final analysis, how everything you have read is activated and maintained. It is the path to your blessings.

We often use the word *"blessings"* casually, without really understanding the power its meaning holds. Let's look, for the moment, at what the biblical term means in the original Greek. There are two Greek words that are translated, *"bless"* or *"blessing."* The first is *"makarios."*[42] It means, *"to be fortunate, well off, happy"* or *"blessed."* The second is *"eulogeo,"*[43] which is used in its verb form to mean, *"to*

---

[42] Strong's number G3107 - *"makarios"* occurs 49 times in the New Testament.
[43] Strong's number G2127 - *"eulogeo"* occurs 42 times as a verb and 15 times as a noun ("a blessing") in the New Testament.

speak well of in a religious way, to thank or invoke a benediction upon a person" or to *"bless, praise."* In its noun form, it means, *"blessing."*

Of all the possible ways we can be blessed, what could be more valuable than being blessed with the Holy Spirit as our Companion and Guide? The Bible tells us, in John 14:17, that Jesus promised the Holy Spirit would not only be with us, but, like Jesus, would abide *"in"* us. The staggering truth this leads us to is that we have God, not only with us, but also in unlimited measure, within us. This is our assurance of all that God has promised. Short of our salvation, it may be the greatest of His assurances. (In fact, it cannot be separated from it.) The Holy Spirit in us becomes our unfailing resource for trust and faith, in spite of anything we face. Here is the promise, in Jesus' own words:

John 3:34 (NKJV)

"For He whom God has sent speaks the words of God, for God does not give the Spirit by measure."

The Purpose of Your Blessing: To Imitate Christ

Why has God sent us the Holy Spirit? What is the purpose of this blessing of having an intimate relationship with Him? The purpose is so we can be more like Jesus.

1 Corinthians 11:1 (NKJV)

"Imitate me, just as I also imitate Christ."

211

There are countless ways to imitate Christ. There is no way to list all of them comprehensively. However, Luke 4:18-19 seem to describe the intent of the Lord's time on earth.

Luke 4:18-19 (NKJV)

"The Spirit of the LORD is upon Me, Because He has anointed Me To preach the gospel to the poor; He has sent Me to heal the brokenhearted, To proclaim liberty to the captives And recovery of sight to the blind, To set at liberty those who are oppressed; {19} To proclaim the acceptable year of the LORD."

Jesus echoed Isaiah's prophecy of more than seven hundred years earlier.

Isaiah 61:1-3 (NKJV)

"The Spirit of the Lord GOD is upon Me, Because the LORD has anointed Me To preach good tidings to the poor; He has sent Me to heal the brokenhearted, To proclaim liberty to the captives, And the opening of the prison to those who are bound; {2} To proclaim the acceptable year of the LORD, And the day of vengeance of our God; To comfort all who mourn, {3} To console those who mourn in Zion, To give them beauty for ashes, The oil of joy for mourning, The garment of praise for the spirit of heaviness; That they may be called trees of righteousness, The planting of the LORD, that He may be glorified."

Fulfilling the Purpose of Your Blessing
(In the Fullness of the Holy Spirit - from Isaiah 61:1-3)

Verse

{1a} *"The Spirit of the Lord GOD is upon Me, Because the LORD has anointed Me To preach good tidings to the poor;"*

This verse holds a double meaning. First, we are obligated to bring the Gospel message to those who are less fortunate and live with a lack of resources for an abundant life. In Matthew 25:40, these are the people Jesus called *"the least of these my brethren."* Second, we are to preach to the *"poor in spirit."* Matthew 5:3 tells us *"...theirs is the kingdom of heaven."* The *"poor in spirit"* are those who live in the spiritual poverty of not knowing Jesus. This category of people has no economic or social boundaries.

{1b} *"He has sent Me to heal the brokenhearted"*

Only God can heal a broken heart, and He has chosen to do it through you. Will you have the compassion to see and respond when the opportunity presents itself?

"To proclaim liberty to the captives, And the opening of the prison to those who are bound;"

God spoke these words metaphorically through the Prophet Isaiah. The prison he spoke of represents the bonds of sin that have captured the world. Notice Isaiah used the word *"proclaim."* This means that we are to proclaim the Gospel and its truths as a way to illuminate the opportunity of salvation through Christ. Then, the Holy Spirit, working through us, will begin the restoration process to bring people into their day of salvation and then, to an eternal lifetime of sanctification.

{2a} *"To proclaim the acceptable year of the LORD, And the day of vengeance of our God;"*

This is the third occurrence of the words *"preach"* or *"proclaim."* God has established a pattern in which we speak the truth of the Gospel. In this case, we are to proclaim that Christ is going to return and will end all sin in His Day of vengeance and judgment. Revelation, Chapters 19 and 20 make this clear. Then, what remains will be acceptable in that it will be holy before the Lord.

{2b - 3a} *"To comfort all who mourn. To console those who mourn in Zion, To give them beauty for ashes, The oil of joy for mourning, The garment of praise for the spirit of heaviness;"*

As with much of Old Testament prophecy, *"those who mourn"* can be interpreted to have a double meaning. First, it can point to those who mourn over the loss of a person or something they valued. Second, it can indicate those who mourn for the loss of God's holiness in the society around them. They mourn for the restoration of God's kingdom. Isaiah assures us that they will exchange ashes for beauty, and put on praise where there was only heaviness.

{3b} "That they may be called trees of righteousness, The planting of the LORD, that He may be glorified."

All that you have read here is the result of the power of the Gospel, which we are called to preach and proclaim. The product of the Gospel process is that those who hear and accept the Gospel will glorify the Lord with the testimonies of their transformed eternal lives. The biblical terms *"trees of righteousness"* and *"the planting of the Lord"* invite us to meditate on Psalms 92:12-15.

Psalms 92:12-15 (NKJV)

"The righteous shall flourish like a palm tree, He shall grow like a cedar in Lebanon. {13} Those who are planted in the house of the LORD Shall flourish in the courts of our God. {14} They shall still bear fruit in old age; They shall be fresh and flourishing, {15} To declare that the LORD is upright; He is my rock, and there is no unrighteousness in Him."

It would be an appropriate ending to this study of Isaiah 61:1-3 to ask you to meditate on what it contains. Then, remember the final words of Isaiah 61:3, *"that He may be glorified."* This is the ultimate purpose of all you have read throughout the book.

Luke 4:18-19 and Isaiah 61:1-3 give us an overview of what Christ has assigned us to do with our blessings. Each of us has a unique part or function in the task, but all of us together are responsible to bring it to pass. This can only

215

happen through the anointing of the Holy Spirit, as we walk with Him through our assigned journeys towards the fulfillment of our destinies. Then, at the appropriate time, which no one knows except the Father, the Kingdom of God will rejoice in the second coming of the Lord Jesus Christ.

As a final thought, read Matthew 5:13-16. When you do what Verse 16 instructs you to do, God will be glorified and the devil will be horrified. You will be walking toward a life of fullness in the Holy Spirit. He will faithfully be in you, for you and with you.

Matthew 5:13-16 (NKJV)

"You are the salt of the earth; but if the salt loses its flavor, how shall it be seasoned? It is then good for nothing but to be thrown out and trampled underfoot by men. {14} You are the light of the world. A city that is set on a hill cannot be hidden. {15} "Nor do they light a lamp and put it under a basket, but on a lampstand, and it gives light to all who are in the house. {16} Let your light so shine before men, that they may see your good works and glorify your Father in heaven."

Now, be blessed to be a blessing. Go and let your light shine before all people at every opportunity. *"They will see your good works and glorify your Father in heaven."*

Dr. Bob Abramson

About Dr. Abramson

Dr. Abramson has extensive experience as a cross-cultural mentor and trainer of those in the five-fold ministry. He and his wife Nancy have pastored international churches in New York City and the Fiji Islands in the South Pacific. He established or taught in Bible schools and ministry training centers in New Zealand, Fiji, Taiwan, Hong Kong, Malaysia, Europe and the United States. He provides free resources worldwide through his website, "Mentoring Ministry" (www.mentoringministry.com).

Dr. Abramson earned a Doctor of Ministry from Erskine Theological Seminary, a Masters in Religion from Liberty University and a Bachelor of Arts in the Bible with a minor in Systematic Theology from Southeastern University. He and his wife Nancy live in Lake Worth, Florida. They have five grown children and seven grandchildren.

Contact Dr. Abramson, at www.mentoringministry.com
or write him at Dr.Bob@mentoringministry.com

Dr. Abramson is also the author of these books.
- "God's Kind of Love"
- "Focused on the Father - The Lord's Prayers"
- "Just a Little Bit More - The Heart of a Mentor" (Book and Workbook)
- "The Leadership Puzzle"

(Two Workbooks and Facilitator's Manual)
- "Growing Together, Marriage Enrichment for Every Culture."
(Book and Workbook)
- "Reflections, Volumes One through Three"
(A Continuing Series of Devotional Journals)
- "Moral Manhood - Swimming with the Sharks"

www.ingramcontent.com/pod-product-compliance
Lightning Source LLC
LaVergne TN
LVHW051506080426
835509LV00017B/1947